MAKING AND THINKING

a study of intelligent activities

Color

HARVESTER STUDIES IN PHILOSOPHY

General Editor: Dr. Margaret Boden, University of Sussex

Also in this series:

Keith Graham
J. L. Austin: A Critique of Ordinary Language Philosophy

Nicholas Bunnin
Self-Deception

Other titles in preparation

MAKING AND THINKING

a study of intelligent activities

ANDREW HARRISON

Lecturer in Philosophy, University of Bristol

THE HARVESTER PRESS

First published in Great Britain in 1978 by
THE HARVESTER PRESS LIMITED
Publisher: John Spiers
2 Stanford Terrace, Hassocks, Sussex

British Library Cataloguing in Publication Data

Harrison, Andrew
Making and thinking.
1. Creative ability
I. Title
153.3′5′01 BF408

ISBN 0–85527–662–2

Printed in Great Britain by
Latimer Trend & Company Ltd Plymouth

Contents

FOR

JOE LEWORTHY

PREFACE

THERE are many people without whom this book would have been difficult, if not impossible, to write. Students at Bristol and elsewhere have provided me with support and encouragement necessary for a conviction that the project might be worth continuing. To Peter Coe of the Department of Architecture, University of Bristol, and to Patrick Johnson I owe a debt for conversations about the arts and philosophy which in the nature of things I cannot estimate. I am indebted to Professor Stephan Körner and Professor Richard Wollheim for having read an earlier draft of my manuscript and for their advice and encouragement; the former I have sometimes taken, the latter I have received with gratitude. Above all I must express my thanks to my wife and family for putting up with my not always good-tempered attempts at getting my thought clear and especially to my wife for her constant endeavours to correct my incorrigibly creative spelling.

ANDREW HARRISON
Bristol, 1978

INTRODUCTION

WE all make things and we all from time to time reflect on and talk about what we and others make. "Making" is among the most general designations we have for intelligent and potentially intelligible activity, yet the question of the sort of intelligible activity making is has received rather less than its due of attention from philosophers who have been ready enough to concern themselves with most other central concepts of human action. Whereas notions such as planning, deciding, recommending, ordering and advising are the common coin of most philosophical enquiries into the place of thought in, or about, what people do, the common terms of the activities of makers of things seem to be far less used and referred to in the philosophical trade. The ideas of designing and constructing (except perhaps in somewhat specialised mathematical and related contexts and senses) figure rarely in the titles of philosophical books and papers, and the no less interesting notions of building, cobbling and bodging not at all. That it can be as much a central mark of intelligence to be able to improvise a useful or decorative artefact from available materials as it is to be able to talk about the problem to others has not generally been seen by philosophers to invite any special sort of enquiry. The tacit concensus seems to be that such things may safely be taken care of by drawing simple consequences from philosophical conclusions about other topics, or else can safely be ignored.

The Aristotelian slogan that man is a rational animal, or more exactly that it should be central to our understanding of people that they may sometimes be significantly charged with irrationality in that sense in which it does not make clear sense to lay the same charge against the activities of mice, lies very properly at the centre of most traditional as well as most recent philosophical accounts of human action. Equally, however, there seems to be a corresponding tendency to assume that that very same distinction may be expressed in the further truism that man is that animal who can talk, that the rationality in question can be understood in terms of, even identified with, the ability to engage in specifically linguistic activities. Since what we may see as dividing us from the beasts we will also be inclined to see as constituting the essential core of our common humanity, this "linguistic chauvinism" (whether justified or not) can very easily incline us to suppose that the best talkers, most cogent language users among us, are at the same time those who most admirably show that central human trait of rationality—are in effect the best people. It is perfectly possible that from such great metaphysical beginnings such little snobberies may grow. We should guard against them.

This is not to say that linguistic competence is not in some way quite central to the very idea of rationality, or of intelligent and intelligible thought in the context of what we do or what we believe. It is merely to say that we should be wary of misinterpreting the place of such a truth in the scheme of things. It can be all too easy, for example, to slide down a slope of verbal associations which might run something as follows.

> We are concerned with rationality and with diagnosing and perhaps curing irrationality. Rationality is a matter of having, or of being able to give, more or less good reasons for what one does or for what one believes. To give reasons is to provide arguments: to be prepared to argue for, or to defend in argument what one believes is or ought to be. It is, accordingly, a matter of being able to argue and hence of being able to debate, talk, and write, a matter of being able to use a language. Hence, if by the claim that man is a rational animal is meant that only such animals may be significantly accused of irrationality, a condition of being such an animal is being able to use a language.

In general, it is not held to be an unacceptable consequence of such a view that a deaf mute, before being taught some sort of a sign language, cannot properly be said to behave on any occasion either rationally or irrationally.

Justified or not, this assimilation of a sort of "human chauvinism" (not of course necessarily a bad thing) to a form of "linguistic chauvinism" is in many ways a characteristic of a specifically *philosophical* tradition in the somewhat restricted sense of such a tradition being bounded by a common debate within the tradition of more or less professional philosophy. Disciplines other than philosophy, though also given to rather grand and uninformative claims about the essential nature of the human animal (at least when introducing themselves to the uninformed) tend to reinforce a specifically linguistic set of criteria by others. Elementary anthropological and palaeontological essays in the more old-fashioned sort of children's encyclopedia have a way of laying at least as much stress on distinguishing early man from other primates in terms of the use of tools and the construction of simple artefacts. There the child may be told that the important thing about men as they evolved into something like ourselves was that they learnt to make knives, pots and shelters, learnt to invent, construct and design things. In such contexts the idea of a maker of things, a tool-user, plays at least as central a role as the idea of a talker or writer. This is, of course, hardly surprising since we can, in the nature of things, have no evidence of the linguistic habits of creatures from the remote past, whereas we do have their pots and axes. We naturally tend to express our prejudices in terms of the data that are nearest to hand.

Of course, "artefact chauvinism' is no more free from problems than its rivals and allies. Birds, beavers, ants, worms and sticklebacks make all sorts of marvellous and elaborate structures. Creatures may even be found that utilise, and even modify, objects as part of the process of making other things, that is to say in some perhaps very minimal sense, they use "tools". Then how does this differ from human building and designing? The simple, and certainly over-simple, thing to say is that such makings are "merely instinctive", that is to say that animals of a certain kind, however elaborate their structures, always stick to the same "blueprint". They may adapt and adopt a variety of materials to make the same sorts of structures, but they do not, or do not significantly, modify the structures. They do not invent, plan or bodge in an emergency, or if they do they learn little or nothing from the success or failure of their bodging. But even this can be a matter of degree, and it is partly for this reason that any radical distinction between man and the beasts can never be *just* a matter of making. For in considering borderline and disputed cases of these sorts we tend quite naturally to ask how far the animal concerned could "really" be supposed to have reflected, speculated and wondered about what it was doing, how far it might "really" have intended to modify the structures involved, or to make use deliberately of the accidents of chance that occurred within the framework of the standard type of artefact. But this is very like asking how the animal might have been thinking at the time, how in a thin, but not vanishingly thin, sense it might have reasoned, and of course we are automatically debarred from that sort of an enquiry so long as we suppose that it just *could* not make sense to ask questions of that sort, to ask them *seriously* outside the context of a language using creature.

Accordingly, we may find ourselves in the situation that the very rigidity of the linguistic picture of rationality succeeds by a kind of default, that is, by not being able to *permit* a serious application of any idea of man-like intelligence in any context where we cannot be sure of language being used. This is surely not the sort of victory of which any theory, philosophical or otherwise, should be proud.

Perhaps the right moral to draw from this is that it is fruitless and empty to engage in speculation so general as that involved in asking what it is that essentially distinguishes man from the beasts. Certainly it is not my question. But even if we were to abandon such an enquiry it is hard to see how we could seriously abandon an interest in such questions as what sorts of things we mean by calling someone intelligent, or sensible, silly, thoughtless, skilful or kack-handed, in other words, about the range of normative expressions we may use concerning the occasions where an agent may take thought in, or about, his actions. And a prejudice in favour of language may give equal trouble here.

If one attempts to explore relationships which may exist between what we have in mind when we ascribe intelligence and intelligibility to someone's making or mending something and his talking, planning, discussing and theorising, one soon discovers that past digging by philosophers has left some artificial scars and discontinuities. The effects of some of these have found their way into the overgrowth of our everyday prejudices and assumptions, just as some of our non-philosophical prejudices have affected what philosophers have had to say. There is no comfortably innocent area of experience and discourse here.

We make, for example, a number of distinctions between what is practical and what is theoretical. Popularly, *practical* sorts of people do things with *things* and make *things*, normally, but not inevitably, running the risk of getting their hands dirty in the process. Popularly, *theoretically* minded people do not do this and do not run these risks. We tend, moreover, to colour these sorts of distinctions with our social attitudes and prejudices. Many of these prejudices have to do with vague notions of intelligence and stupidity about which philosophers ought perhaps to be more inquisitive than they sometimes are. Perhaps their lack of curiosity is not altogether surprising since on the whole professional academics tend to benefit from them. Schoolmasters still tend to place those children who are on the whole rather good at arguing and disputing, who have a good command of language, in the "higher" "A" streams of their schools, while those who are rather better at making things (material things, that is) tend to be placed in classes that are named by letters further down the alphabet. (I am, of course, well aware that yet other schoolmasters are inclined to invert their snobberies at this point.) Our prejudices are that rude mechanicals will be rather rude, and civil engineers less civil than historians. Generally speaking, when a school report describes a child as "somewhat more practically inclined" the implication is that he would do better to develop his talent for making chairs, not that he would do well to attempt to enter a profession where his skill in moral argument can more fully be made use of. There may even yet be occasions where to describe someone as a practical sort of person is little more than a tactful way of saying that he is virtually incapable of reflecting on, or deciding anything verbally and "in the abstract".

By contrast, the writer of such a report might well be forgiven for finding a philosophical discussion of "practical reason" a somewhat bewildering experience. On the face of it this particular piece of philosophical terminology seems to derive from Kant, though it is pretty clear that the source is both wider and deeper than one philosopher. Kant's second critique, *The Critique of Practical Reason* is, of course, centrally concerned with moral thinking, and of course, despite the terminology of the schoolmaster's report, moral thinking *is* inevitably practical since it is concerned with how people should *behave*, and with what they had better *do*, rather than with how they should think, and with what they had better *believe*. However, in line with this terminology, most philosophical discussions of practical reasoning tend to confine themselves to problems about thinking in moral, or perhaps legal or political, situations, and to consider very little, if at all, the sorts of thinking that can be involved in more mundanely practical contexts. The overwhelming majority of discussions in such contexts seems to be concerned with administrative rather than with executive thinking.

It can be a somewhat unnerving experience to attend a philosophical discussion on the nature of "practical reason" while preoccupied with the relatively straightforward practical problem of how to repair an awkwardly broken window or a chair. There can seem to be very little relation indeed between the topics being discussed around one and the passage of reflection one is engaged in, or may subsequently become engaged in with one's hands full of glass and putty. Even the suggestion that it should have such a relevance can come to seem a sort of intellectual bad form. Certainly, the very style of the Kantian context of the idea of practical reason is hardly suggestive of any situation where one may run the risk of getting dirt under the fingernails. Reason, however practical, suggests a world of Thought more readily than one of messing around with materials. Perhaps this is right and natural since the proper context of reason—that context in which that rather abstract and rarefied noun can find vigorous life—*is* that of reasoning, giving and having reasons, thinking and concluding. So it may seem wholly natural to suppose (reasonable, even) that someone actually engaged in, absorbed in, and concentrating on a practical task has either left the time for such reflection behind him, or has no need of it.

This seems to me to be a mistake, and partly, though not wholly, a mistake of philosophical style. What I mean by that is that while it is clear enough that many errors in philosophy, as in any other discipline, may derive from errors of inference, from deriving the wrong conclusions from available premises, by no means all do and it can be a misunderstanding of the nature of the subject to suppose that because philosophers are, of all people, professionally concerned with arguments and the analysis of arguments, philosophical error is standardly error in argument. The converse may equally apply: it is remarkable how a philosophical commentator on a major thinker from the past may be prepared to claim both that his subject was a great and important contributor to the progress of human understanding while at the same time apparently find fault with the majority of that thinker's central arguments. Though this may sometimes bewilder students, such a position is perfectly consistent and right since it may just be that the contribution made by his subject consisted of persuading himself and those who were inclined to either agree or disagree with him that hitherto neglected topics were interesting and important. Contrary to a well-known Austinian slogan, importance is of the greatest importance in philosophy. Philosophical style is very much a matter of what may become suggested as important and central, and what may be suggested, in each case normally tacitly, as unimportant, peripheral and uninteresting.

My suggestion is, then, that the problems of practical thinking with quite mundane sorts of things and stuff, that find expression in what is done with those materials, have suffered from this sort of stylistic neglect. Such neglect has in consequence distorted our understanding of other sorts of thinking and of other, perhaps more sophisticated, sorts of thought in action.

One such more sophisticated area has to do with the arts. The making of a work of art, whatever else it may be, involves the construction of an artefact that is a vehicle for thought, at least in that general sense in which such objects demand our understanding and interpretation, and in doing so demand at the same time from us an understanding of the maker of them—in some sense or other, a sense that is neither perfectly clear nor, certainly, free from philosophical difficulties, they are objects of communication.

In an essay on the "historical function of the museum", the critic, John Berger, attacked what he saw as the almost universal tendency of those who value or have charge of paintings to see them primarily as property objects and only secondarily as objects of a different sort of significance.

> "It is necessary," he said, "to make an imaginative effort that runs contrary to the whole contemporary trend in the art world: it is necessary to see works of art freed from all the mystique that attaches to them as property objects. It then becomes possible to see them as testimony to the process of their own making instead of as products; to see them in terms of action instead of finished achievement. The question 'What went into the making of this?' supercedes the collector's question of 'What is this?' " (John Berger, *The Moment of Cubism,* Weidenfeld and Nicholson, p. 35.)

Painting, more than the other arts, suffers from that sort of confusion of values that is the object of Berger's complaint, for the objects made by painters are unique particular material objects. Therefore, like stamps or rare manuscripts, they may be collected, bought and sold. Famous paintings of the sort that are housed in museums are notoriously valuable items, and one need understand nothing of the process of painting or of what paintings may be able to show us or convey to be impressed by the money they represent. Whereas a collector of rare manuscripts does not thereby buy and sell the poems they are manuscripts of, a collector of paintings owns and disposes of the works of art themselves, for it is as if paintings, considered as an analogy with books as a form of communication, were identical with their own manuscripts. It is thus a predicament for anyone who is concerned to judge and interpret paintings, in a way in which it is not for critics of the other arts, to guard against that tendency which at its crudest is shown in the tourist who sees the *Mona Lisa* as a million dollars and not as a painting demanding judgement and attention. Perhaps this predicament is obvious and familiar, and certainly there would seem to be nothing especially new or "contemporary" about it. But the issues underlying it are none the less important and pressing. Some are clearly social and political, but others are conceptual, are concerned with some of our most fundamental ideas of significance and the significant products of action. They are by no means confined to the philosophy of art.

Why, for example, do we regard paintings, as we do not regard poems, as identical with their own manuscripts? One possible answer might be that verbal artefacts, such as poems can be said to have a significance—that is to say a linguistic sense—in a far more clear and precise sense of the word than that applicable to other made things. A poem is not its inscription because its sense is not, any more than the word "poem" in the English language is to be identified with all or any of its inscriptions. As we shall see that is a partial answer, but is not, and could not be the whole of the answer. However, that it may be a part of an answer, or at least relevant to an answer can indicate a deeper, primary issue. Berger quite properly says of a painting that it may be "a testimony to the process of its own making", but what does this mean? Does such an expression refer merely to the fact that we may find out in some way by studying the object how it was put together, how we might proceed were we to wish to make something like it, or does it refer to something else, perhaps to how the painter thought when he made it, how the activity of making expressed what he thought? To understand what someone is saying is, whatever else may be involved, to understand *him*. Might there be a parallel manner in which to understand a picture that someone has made is similarly to understand *him*? But what would such a view really amount to? There surely must be some sense in which to say such a thing is to say something both true and important. What is by no means as clear is that we can be quite sure what truth we are thereby concerned with and why it may be important.

The issue, however, is considerably wider than the arts, and certainly wider than the pictorial arts, for it raises the question what in general we might mean by the "process" of making if we consider it as a form of intelligible activity. Making may be inventive, creative, original. It may also be the reverse of these things, slavish, dull and boring. These are ascriptions of thought and action. It is people who think, attend and act in various ways, or who fail to think, fail to attend in what they do who may be praised for their originality and their inventiveness, or condemned for their dullness. Such ascriptions are, moreover, central to much of what we care most about in human affairs. They are concerned with the ability that we may have or fail to have to contribute what is new rather than with passing on what already is, or with passively reacting. In a central, if not altogether clear, sense they are concerned with activity in the sense that to act may be contrasted with re-acting. The central contention that I shall be pursuing is that that sense of action is irreducibly concerned with making.

I have said that on the whole philosophers have neglected the idea of making things in their concern with the ideas of action. Insofar as they have done so they have, I believe, left out of account the most central concept of action that we can have. An account of action that does not include an account of the action of making *can,* it seems to me at best only be an account of action's periphery.

This is because the philosophically puzzling notion of creativity—of making things new—lies at the heart of the matter of intelligent activity. In many ways it is the skeleton in the cupboard for most of our traditional theories and attitudes concerning the very idea of rational, intelligent and intelligible activity. By no means all such theories and attitudes are "philosophical" theories in a narrow professional sense of that word, though they all have philosophical roots some exhibit themselves in quite everyday social prejudices. In many ways it is these attitudes that go to make our thinking about what it is to act creatively, to create something, radically unclear. This unclarity expresses itself in two sorts of closely connected ways. On the one hand we tend to project the unclarity of our thinking in these matters on to their topic, to assume either that creativity is essentially irrational or, more honorifically, non-rational or even superrational. In this manner we talk of mysterious flair and inspiration in a maker's creativity. On the other hand we tend to suppose that such matters have not only much to do with the arts, but can be of interest only in that context. In many ways the idea that the arts are special and peculiar, that the activities and experiences of artists are not like those of other men, and that the philosophical questions we may ask about such things can be safely confined within "aesthetics" can be seen as a response to the scandal of creativity. It is a scandal of neglect and embarrassment, and it is no less a scandal in so far as the cupboard in which the family skeleton is confined is a prettily gilded one. My underlying contention in what follows is that this state of affairs not only can be remedied, but that we have an urgent need to begin on the remedy. We can do so, I believe, by setting the matter of making at the centre of our view of action.

This may seem to imply a bold claim. It is intended to imply a modest one. I have not in what follows established any firm or proven thesis concerning action and thought. There are few detailed analyses and there are certainly no proofs. I am not sure that this is a defect that I could in principle remedy however. What argument I have is in the form not of a thesis or a proof, but of a plea that certain issues (some of them, but by no means all, concerned with the philosophy of art), should be considered as central that have hitherto tended to be regarded as peripheral, and conversely that certain other issues that have often been regarded as of paramount importance should be set slightly to one side. My later and in many ways more detailed discussions (mostly in the final three chapters) *are* concerned with topics in the philosophy of art, and in that sense are "about" aesthetics, but neither there, nor in this study as a whole, is that department of philosophical inquiry that I am concerned with except in so far as I am attempting to show that there can be no such separate department of our inquiries. What does seem to be quite clearly the case, however, is that certain quite general features of our thought and action are exhibited most clearly and intelligibly in the context of the arts and that we neglect them at our peril. What this study is about is the place of thought in the activities of making things in which we may all of us engage, and in so far as I have a more specific topic than that, it is the topic of creating, of making what is new, what goes beyond pre-established aims, principles or rules for action, and with why we may have got ourselves into the predicament of that being hard to make sense of.

And that topic is a very general one, whether it is concerned with God creating a universe, a painter a picture, or with new thought and action in moral or political contexts. To most of that general area it has only been possible to pay fairly cursory attention, but even that may serve the purpose of showing that something may be visible that has hitherto been kept hidden or thought invisible. What follows is concerned to plead for a new angle of view. I have been able at best to sketch, and certainly not to draw in detail, the landscape so revealed.

Much of this landscape will be familiar. To find fault, as I do, with an all-pervasive means-end picture of rationality is a theme of much libertarian and Romantic thought. My insistence on the central role of attention in the idea of intelligent activity owes something to Ryle, though its strategy at least is different, just as my account of making pictures owes a debt to Gombrich which any modern writer on aesthetics must own. Other philosophers I have acknowledged, many others I should have done. Taken on their own few of my moral and political comments will seem very new. However, what can matter is the order in which one traverses an area. The route I take is to begin with the grammar of certain elementary claims about making things in order to outline as my main theme a central sense of making in which the maker's concept of the object he is making emerges from his understanding of what he does with his materials, to consider the social and moral context of this idea, and from there to offer an account, not merely of intelligent attention, but of its *structure* that can be placed at the centre of our view of intelligent action. From there I turn by way of the idea of picturing, which should be seen, as others have seen it, as a heuristic paradigm of a form of thought, to indicate how our perspective on other areas of philosophy may be seen from that viewpoint. Thus, the centre of my account is simply that; and is neither a premise nor a conclusion.

CHAPTER ONE

MAKING AND THE PROCESS OF MAKING

MAKING things is, or at least can be, a rational activity. That is to say to make something may be to do something that is informed by thought, where thought, reflection, knowledge and speculation may have its outcome in doing. So the matter of making is part of that general philosophical area that is often called the philosophy of action. Moreover, making things, like other sorts of action and activities, changes the world, and it changes the world specifically by bringing into existence objects, entities of some sort that were not in existence before. However, this ghost of a definition is open to some immediate and obvious difficulties. I can certainly change the world, even bring something into existence in the world that was not present before, but unintentionally, inadvertently, or quite absent-mindedly. My children have made a hole in the wallpaper by leaning their stilts against it, and I frequently ask them to make less noise. But the noise they make is not something that they have made, and the hole in the wallpaper is not the outcome of any activity of making something. In the former case we do not have to do with a thing, a made object, an artefact, in the latter no deliberate constructive activity. But what do we mean by these things? How does the idea of making relate the two?

When after the first day at school my children proudly return home carrying the things that they have made, strange constructions of cardboard and paint, is there any sense at all in saying that what they have with them is the outcome of a "rational activity"? Surely this is to crush their fragile success with crippling honours? Yet they have made *something*, and they have *made* it, and it is important to them that they have.

Quite inanimate agencies can well be said to make things. The melting snow can make a mess of the pavement, the burning cake of the inside of the oven. The waves can make images of themselves on the hitherto smooth sand—cause there to be things that were not there before. It would seem to be inevitable with any topic that is concerned with human action, rational or otherwise, that there will always run alongside any notions of human, rational, or animate agency, a "thinner" set of possibilities concerned with inanimate agency or responsibility. It is hard to see how this could fail to be so since the mechanisms by which we can effect changes in the world inevitably involve that sort of bodily agency that may occur without our responsibility. We are, whatever else we may be, material bodies dealing with other material bodies, hence any account of sentient responsibility must assume a background account of simple material responsibility. Complexities here are not *specially* concerned with the topic of making. These are general problems concerning the place of thought in, or the absence of thought in, any action or activity. But what is more specifically concerned with the matter of making has to do with what we should say about the place of thought in a child's making something if "rational activity" does seem to be ponderous and out of place.

Anyone who has seen the careful concern with which children make the things they do, the concentration and contemplation that accompanies their activities, would be hard put to claim that no mental activity was involved or that it was not intimately connected with the very idea of bringing something quite specific into being. But what might be claimed here and what denied? Is it a matter of planning, of assessing, of inferring, of reasoning or calculating? None of these things seems to be quite the right things to say, and yet clearly they are not quite out of place either. All these things seem to impose a weight of interpretation that the story will not bear, yet there can be good reasons to suppose that they are of the utmost relevance: they are the typical acts of rational beings, marking the animate side of any animate/inanimate distinction, and even a child making a not very recognisable dragon out of a toilet roll is very clearly on the human side of that fence. However, if there are difficulties about these expressions in this context, there are some things that we can say for certain. One is that the child is proud of having made *something*. This is not the same thing as simply proudly doing something. We are being asked to admire an artefact, not, or not merely, a performance.

Recall how a child behaves when building sandcastles on a beach, for the difference between building sandcastles and merely playing with sand can show as much in the child's behaviour as in its outcome. In the former case his quite characteristic activity is to stop what he is doing from time to time and contemplate what he has done: what he is doing is watching something, a castle, a dam, a harbour, growing out of what he has done with the sand, new identities emerging from the changes produced in the materials. Objects emerge from chaos. What might we mean by the claim that to make in the relevant sense is to make *something*?

English, in common with many other languages, does not seem to make any very clear terminological distinction between making and doing. This is not to say that it makes no distinction at all (English children when being taught French are frequently told that the verb "faire" can be translated by "make or do", which at least suggests that they can be assumed to recognise that there are some options here) but such differences show themselves in contexts rather than in the bare vocabulary. At all events, whereas to make a cake is to have made something, to make love, or a great deal of noise, or to make someone very happy is not. While a child home from school could express the very same thought in showing us his toilet roll dragon by saying "Look what I did!" as by saying "Look what I made!", that thought is concerned unambiguously with making as opposed to doing in that what he is proudly claiming to be responsible for is an object rather than a mere state of affairs. And this is a logical distinction. Moreover it is fundamental.

Any sort of agency clearly brings it about that some fact about the world is that was not before, making brings it about that some individual exists that was not before. Not all changes introduce new individuals, but (divine creation *ex nihilo*, if there can be such a thing, apart) any action that involves the coming into being of some new thing will surely involve at the same time changes in things, or in the conditions of things. Making is a species of doing. But to say this raises more questions than it answers. Is making jam making *something*? Is making a mess? Is making a heap of rubbish out of what was once a brick wall making something? Similar questions might be asked about what is meant by the concomitant condition that to make something is also to change something (something else?) in the process. Is this a necessary condition of making?

However, these do seem to me to be the right and natural questions to ask at the start of any enquiry into the philosophical psychology of verbs of making, since they are concerned with the twin ideas of a finished product, and of using materials in its construction. Questions of this sort are frequently asked in the contexts of general theories of design and aesthetics as if they had to do with such things as the theory and practice of good workmanship: it is well to insist that in their most general form they have to do with the logic of these concepts of action.

On the whole it does seem reasonably clear that simply to rearrange a heap of stones or bricks into a slightly differently ordered pile is *merely* to alter the configuration of the pile. This could conceivably prompt some intellectual puritan to maintain that the building walls or houses was then equally "merely" altering one heap or pile of material found in the builder's yard into another of a different configuration on the building site. Hence, he might conclude, if one knocks over a wall so that the stones are once again a heap of rubble, one has "made" something, the heap, in just as full a sense as if one had "made" a wall out of the pile of stones. And that full sense is of course a pretty empty one. But this is a perverse argument, as all arguments are that trade on the word "merely" to argue that there is no significant difference between a case one side of a given borderline case and one on the other. Some walls are indeed so "slung up with a shovel" that there may be little to choose between them and heaps, between building them and knocking things down, but nothing of great interest follows from that about either building or buildings.

What is it that is so odd about an exchange such as the following said seriously? A child returns from school and we ask him what he did today,

"We had handwork, and we all made things. Tommy made a clown out of scraps, and I made a great big mess all over the art room floor, and making my thing took a lot more scraps than Tommy used."

Of course we might just suppose that he had misunderstood the teacher's instructions, whatever they were (the philosophically lazy trick when faced with an odd example of verbal or other behaviour of supposing just any unspecified misunderstanding on the part of the agent is an infallible recipe for losing chances to use our conceptual imagination) but suppose his misunderstanding was minimal and that the teacher told the children to see what they could make. Would we not at least have to suppose a (certainly perverse and unusual) pride in the fact that the result was the outcome of what he did, and that he really worked at the business of producing it? Of course we do not normally regard chaos and confusion as worth producing, or if so requiring to be worked on. But if we did might we not have vandal-craftsmen, good at their trade?

In other words, there really does seem to be a link between the idea of making *something*—how far we may be tempted to regard the outcome of the activity as an identifiable entity—and the sort of value we may be prepared to place on the activity of producing it. Is this merely an illusion?

There are many cases where marking the difference between making in the relevant sense and doing is more straightforward. One thing that Tommy did that day at school was make the teacher happy (by making such a good clown), while what he made was a clown which he subsequently gave to the teacher. In "Tommy made her clown" the expression "her clown" can then subsequently be used to answer the question what it was that he made whereas "her happy" clearly cannot for the very good reason that "her happy" could not be used to answer *any* question. The object of the active verb in "Tommy made a clown" can become the subject of a corresponding passive verb in "a clown was made by Tommy". Not being a noun phrase "her happy" could never be used to answer any question what, who, which was it that . . .? This may certainly show why it may be somehow right to say that what is made is *things* (what noun phrases refer to, perhaps), but it is still too easy.

It is too easy because if we are not careful it can look as if the claim that Tommy made a clown expresses some sort of a relation between Tommy and that clown of which he was so proud. But it is by no means clear that in making the clown out of scraps he did anything to it at all: it was only when he was finished and done that there was a clown. Before that whatever it was that Tommy was doing was not being done to the clown he made. This may seem to be somewhat of a quibble, but it is none the less worth pursuing.

As I hope to make clear as this account proceeds, the ways in which thought may be exercised, or expressed in, the activities of making things have very largely to do with how the maker relates his thought and his actions to on the one hand his *materials* and on the other to the object itself that he is making. The latter, while importantly an "object" in the sense of being a "thing" is at the same time "the object of" his activity, but, of course, the materials of which that thing will, if the maker is successful be made, will also be "objects of" his attention in his activity of making. The various connections and distinctions here are in an important sense what the philosophical problem of making is all about. On the face of it the matter would seem to be in this way fairly straightforward, for it would, after all seem to be the truth and very nearly the whole truth that whatever is made by someone will be made of whatever materials he uses. But while this may even be very nearly the whole truth it is by no means a simple truth, and to be very nearly the whole truth is not to be *quite* the whole of the matter. What may seem to be tedious complications at this stage may well turn out to be hair-line cracks that mark the beginnings of quite large fissures in the fabric of that simple story.

We might impatiently shrug off the quibble here by saying that, well, what is *meant* by the claim that Tommy made a clown is that in doing whatever it was that he did to the scraps and bits of stuff his teacher gave him they got made into a clown, that what he did was to make those scraps clown-like. What else could he have done? The matter of referring to that clown that he made might then be regarded as just another way of compendiously referring to the clown-like condition of the scraps which was the outcome of Tommy's afternoon work. And on this account his afternoon's work consisted in changing the condition of certain scraps and bits of stuff. But, of course, Tommy's day of good deeds continued a little longer than that. He concluded the business by making his teacher happy by presenting the clown he had made to her, altering her emotional condition by making her happy that way as he had previously altered the material condition of the stuff he had been working on. But now why can't we describe every part of the story in terms of Tommy simply as an agent of change in each case? Hasn't the distinction we are seeking collapsed?

Of course, we still have that noun phrase, "the clown that Tommy made", but is this really a problem? Noun phrases are easily enough constructed. Tommy was responsible for the clown, but there was something else that he was responsible for too, namely his teacher's happiness on that depressing day when the other children made such a mess. Certainly, we are not so free with expressions like "teacher's happiness" or the "traveller's joy" as we are with "Tommy's clown" or "the house that Jack built", but why should this not be the merest quirk of stylistic usage? If we are happy to talk of the teacher's books and sweaters, why not the joys of the teacher?

One answer might run as follows: Tommy may, of course, both be the agent responsible for there being a clown and the agent of his teacher's happiness, and if it is true that he brought it about that a clown existed, and that is all we know about the matter, at least we can say *that* though that may be the most we can say. On the other hand, if he was responsible for his teacher's happiness or her distress, rage or boredom, knowing that we must know as well that there was such a teacher to be bored, enraged or cheered up. Expressions such as "the joys of Mary", or "the perils of Pauline" make an internal, "essential" reference to Pauline and Mary in a way that "the house that Jack built", or "the perils of Pauline" do not. It is, in other words, a logical presupposition of these latter claims that there should have already been a teacher for Tommy to make happy, whereas it is just not a logical presupposition of the claim that he made a clown that there should have been a clown for him to make. We might express this by saying that the logical schema that most naturally fits "A made a B" is,

A brought it about that there was something that was a B.

A brought it about that (Ex) (x was a B)

whereas, by contrast the natural schema for the straightforward claim that A brought about a change in B is,

There was a B that A made f.

(Ex) (x was B and A brought it about that B became f)

and this follows from just those considerations that seemed to involve a quibble, namely that there very well might not have been the clown that Tommy made until he had managed to make it. This may seem to provide the first indications of a firm basis for a distinction between making something and other sorts of agency.

On the other hand it does not seem to be, surely could not be, a *logical* condition of Tommy's making that clown that those bits and pieces of material should have been altered by him the way that they were. This was indeed a *causal* condition of his making the thing, and it surely, for just that reason, has to be a contingent matter that that was how he achieved his result. At all events, it surely would not be contradictory to suppose that he might have made the clown some other way, out of some other, perhaps very similar materials, or even (since logical considerations should not rule out magic) by just snapping his fingers? To be sure he would not have then made a clown-out-of-the-scraps-his-teacher-gave-him, but could he not still have made the clown?

A sculptor's making his sculpture (Michaelangelo carving David) is sometimes referred to in terms of his transforming a piece of marble, or making it *into*, a statue. There are many obscurities here, but it is important to distinguish two quite distinct claims that can be expressed by these sorts of phrases. One such refers to the sculptor's bringing it about that some particular piece of stone, clay or wood became a statue, portrait, bust or whatever. The other may more restrictedly claim that he caused there to be such a bust, statue and so on of wood, clay, stone etc. The two sorts of claims are *logically* distinct in the sense that the sculptor's being responsible for there being a sculpture of a certain sort,

M was responsible for (Ex) (x was a sculpture with such and such properties),

does not entail that of certain materials it was the case that the sculptor was responsible for their becoming such and such a statue,

(Ex) (M was responsible for x becoming D).

We might label this distinction by saying that the latter refer to the *process* of a sculptor's making, while the former refers to the fact simply that he was responsible for there being such a sculpture. The relation between the two sorts of claims are in some way fundamental to the matter of making.

We might see how far this is so by considering the most elevated conception of making that we might have, namely, the idea of God's making—"creating"—a world. Running through the history of, at all events European, thought about making is the feeling that in making something a craftsman or an artist can share in something of the condition of the divine, of the relation of Creator to creature. But what is that relation? Is it even a relation at all? As we shall see, the urge to pay such metaphysical, even mystical, compliments to ourselves as makers of things has a great deal to do with the intellectual predicament that the very idea of making and of the sort of practical thinking that may be involved therein can present to us. We often express such a feeling that there must be something in the matter of making that is transcendental to the normal business of thought and activity by talking of a maker's "inspiration", his "flair", and revealingly, his "creativity". These wider and in many ways vaguer, implications and suggestions are both important and deeply embedded in our thought about ourselves, but before turning to examine them it is well to see that there can be a preliminary set of *logical* questions which we might ask compendiously by asking what it is that we do mean by the relation a maker has to his artifact, of a Creator to his creatures, or of a sculptor to his sculpture? Should we talk in the latter case of his responsibility for there being a sculpture of a certain sort or to the process of his making it?

Geach in his discussion of divine creation *ex nihilo* appeals to very much this distinction.[1] For the problem of how it can make sense to suppose some agent such as God making the world yet needing not to have to use some materials for doing so, would seem to be directly answered by a formulation of this sort. That A brought it about that (Ex) (x was a B) is clearly logically consistent with a claim that A was not responsible for anything (any materials used in the making of B) becoming B. It does not follow from the claim that,

God brought it about that (Ex) (x is an A)

that,

(Ex) (God brought it about that x is an A):

Another way of putting this might be to say that any conviction that we may have that one cannot make anything out of nothing is, along with more specific convictions such as that one cannot make bricks without straw, part of our more or less fundamental *causal* assumptions, and not part of our fundamental *logical* assumptions. If, as those theological sceptics among us may suppose, it is ridiculous to think of anything being created out of nothing at all, our difficulties are not that to claim so is as it stands directly contradictory. Be that as it may, however, Geach is surely right in pointing to the distinction between the two claims, and in arguing as he does that the difference has to do with two different ways of binding the "x" in the formulae. It would however be misleading to conclude from the context of Geach's account that the issue has only to do with the logic of theological or cosmological topics. The heart of the matter is making, whether by God of the Creation, or by a child with his sandcastles.

It might seem that the very thin claim merely that some agent had made something, made in such a way as to commit the speaker to nothing about the process of his doing so, could, at all events outside the above rarefied and specialised contexts, be taken to be of vanishing interest. We do, after all, normally assume that some process (in my sense) was involved. Moreover, the claim that someone responsible for bringing it about that something or other became an A, certainly does seem to imply that that person made an A. To take Geach's examples, that

(Ex) (God brought it about that x is an A) does imply, even though it is not implied by, the claim that God brought it about that (Ex) (x is an A), so, except when we have this very special case of God's responsibility in mind, why should we not in practice always be taken to be making the more compendious of the two claims? Could we ever have occasion *just* to claim that someone was responsible for something's having come into being as an A? But even if this is so it by no means follows that the distinction is unimportant in these more ordinary contexts.

The propusition that some agent brought something *to be an A* is by no means as clear as it might be. At first sight it might seem that the difference between making something and changing something, between making a chair and painting it red, could be brought out by contrasting the claims,

A was responsible for making x f

and

A was responsible for making x to be a B.

But English idiom is notoriously ambiguous here. A well-known exchange of graffiti runs, "My mother made me a queer."—"If I gave her the wool would she make me one too?" The report that attending Professor X's lectures made Jones a cynical rebel, neither means, clearly enough, that the professor made a cynical rebel for Jones, nor, normally, that the professor made a cynical rebel, namely Jones, but simply that those lectures of his made Jones cynically rebellious. But we could report that the professor made a cynical rebel who happened to be Jones, too, and mean something significantly *different* from the *mere* report that as a result of the professor's methods Jones got taken that way.

It would be a matter of the professor's intentions. If we exclude the most likely possibility that the effects on Jones were quite unintentional on the professor's part, and suppose them to have been the outcome of some devious and deliberate educational design, there are then two alternatives. On the one hand, we might imagine him faced with the depressingly conservative Jones and thinking that it would be very much better if he could at least be a little like the other students, deliberately setting to work on him. On the other we might suppose the frustrated lecturer wishing that there might at all events be just one rebel among the lumpen congregation, and setting to work on the nearest material to hand, who happened to be the unfortunate Jones. The first fantasy then has the agent of Jones's corruption having the intention that would naturally fit into the schematic form,

I am endeavouring that (Ex) (x shall become a cynical rebel)

and the latter,

(Ex) (I am endeavouring that x shall become a cynical rebel)

which distinction is clearly in line with the ones we have already noted. (Any oddity here would seem to derive solely from the unlikely educational assumptions involved in the example.) It is then natural enough to say that in the latter case it is, while in the former it is not, a sort of an accident that it is *Jones* who is the object of the policy of making a cynical rebel.

Just such an analogy is noted by Geach between the claims that God brought it about that (Ex) (x is an A) and that (Ex) (God brought it about that x is an A) and an ambiguity in the intentional statement "I am looking for a detective story." He notes that though this ambiguity is often explained by saying that while on the one hand I may mean that I am looking for a particular detective story, while on the other I may mean some detective story or other, this explanation is logically lame since any detective story is some detective story or other and any detective story is also a particular detective story. His explanation is to distinguish between two ways in which the claim that I am endeavouring that it may be the case that I find x and x is a detective story may be true, those facts that may be separately expressed by saying either "I am endeavouring that it may be the case that (Ex) (I find x, and x is a detective story)" and "(Ex) (I am endeavouring that I find x and x is a detective story)." He points out that the logical relations between these two pairs exactly parallel those between the two pairs he has previously considered concerning God's making something, in that in this case the former statement may be true while the latter is false while we are equally not committed to the view that there *was* something *that* God made to be whatever it was on the premise that God was responsible for the being of whatever it was. All of which is, even if a trifle tedious, plain enough sailing.

What is, however, neither so tedious nor such plain sailing is the conclusion that Geach draws from this, which is that "just as 'God created an A' does not assert a relation of God to an A, so 'I am looking for a detective story' does not assert a relation of myself to a detective story." Clearly enough on at least one reasonable interpretation of someone's looking for something there is no relation asserted between him and whatever he is looking for, since that he is doing so is sadly compatible with the non-existence of the object of his search. (Witch-hunting never made witches.) But this could not be the explanation of a similar claim in the case of God and whoever it may be that God is responsible for: if God of all agents, is responsible for the existence of A, then A most certainly exists. Moreover, we might have supposed that of all imaginable relations none could be so close, secure and intimate as that between an object and the agent of its making, or of creator to creature. Could there be any reason to deny something so natural? Such a view would surely have serious consequences for any sort of making as well as for creating in this special sense.

In other words, if a reason for saying that these statements do not assert a relation between the respective agents and the objects of their actions depends simply on their supposed compatability with the non-existence of the objects concerned, Geach's claim is false and obviously false. Perhaps we should look a little further.

In the first place, we might note that while Geach is obviously right in his rejection of the particular "vernacular" explanation he refers to the difference between the two ways in which one may be said to be looking for a detective story, it does seem that we might offer a different "vernacular" explanation of that difference that would not be as obviously faulty. This would be to say that where "I am looking for a detective story" is taken to mean that just *any* detective story will do for me so long as I find one, it will be a kind of accident that that story that I do succeed in finding is the one that satisfies me, whereas in the case that "a detective story" refers to some specific story that I have in mind it will not be. To point out that any story will be some particular story, and that any particular story will be some story or other, is while true enough, quite irrelevant to the fact that my intentions may differ in this way. Sometimes I just want to read something (more or less anything will do, I am not particular) and sometimes it is a particular book that I have in mind. It can be just possible to be misled by English idiom here, since one idiomatic way of expressing just how particular I am about my reading matter is for me to say that there is a story that I have in mind that I particularly want to read. This could just possibly give the misleading impression that to say that asserts that there exists such a story, and that I have it in mind to read it.

Of course that idiom asserts nothing of the kind. One might for instance, say that there is a particular story that I want to write. I do not want to write any old story, though it is very unlikely that it will ever get written: the idiom merely expresses the fact that I have a very precise idea of what will count for me as success were I to achieve it. In no way would saying that be equivalent to asserting that (Ex) (x is a story and I want to write x). So even this somewhat modified "vernacular" explanation will certainly not do to identify the distinction that Geach has in mind. But it does identify an important distinction nonetheless: it is that in some reports of successful finding, or making or writing "that is the story I was looking for", or "that is what I was trying to make" refers to something precise that I did have in mind, while in others it does not.

While there may well be a possible sense of "I am looking for A" that we might construe as (Ex) (x is A and I am looking for x), the statement "(Ex) (x is A and I am endeavouring to make x)" seems to make no sense at all. If something or other is what I am trying to make, that, at the very best, is not yet. Moreover, if looking for something is not a matter of bringing something into being, making essentially is. Accordingly, there would seem to be something quite misleading in an attempt to find a parallel between the logic of statements about making, or creating, and seductively more familiar statements about looking and seeking, at least as far as such a supposed parallel is concerned with existence and not with what it is to have "something in mind". And *that* last issue *is* central to the matter of making; in many ways it is the theme of what I shall be concerned with later. Meanwhile, it is as well to get the question of existence as far as possible out of the way, at all events as a beginning.

The main interest of the idea of creation *ex nihilo* in the context of making generally is simply that it seems to provide a, perhaps weird, limiting case of that sort of making where materials are not involved. In traditional discussions of "theological logic" the sort of questions raised by such creation are for instance "Is creation a change?". As Prior[2] puts the matter, paraphrasing Aquinas, one natural answer to that question of what creation is, is to say (if we can make sense of the idea of creation at all) "that the world was made out of nothing just *means that it wasn't made out of anything*". Accordingly, to quote Prior, that X was created can be expressed by saying "Once X was not, and now is [and that] cannot mean 'Once X's not-being was the case and now its being is', but can only mean 'It is *not* the case that X *was* but it *is* the case that X *is*,' and this does not express a change but two contrasting present facts". One part of this point that we can surely readily accept is that at least that X was created does not report a change in X, and of course if X is the world, i.e. everything, then not a change in anything at all. Perhaps if X is not the whole world some change may be reported none the less. Not only God can create things in the sense of bringing things into being without using materials in the process. Queen Anne created baronies: *they* were not changed thereby, but we might well think that the world was significantly altered by their addition. So, is the point to be that in cases of creation *what is made* is not thereby subjected to change?

Geach's point about creating turns on the thesis that to say of God that he caused it to be the case that (Ex) (x is an A) does not entail that something was made to be an A. But what would this amount to anyway? What is intended is clearly enough that nothing, no materials, no previously existing stuff, had to be used by God in the process of bringing A into being. Since it is also part of Geach's thesis that in creating A God is not in some relation, presumably some sort of a causal relation, to A, it would seem to follow that such a causal relation of the sort that does hold in normal making is naturally expressed by saying of something that it was made *to be* something else. This tacit account of normal making is it seems to me, obscure.

Let us suppose that someone makes a more or less elaborate carving on the central panel of a door, that the carving is carved into the panel that was already there. Obviously in any standard sense of having made an artefact the carver has done this. But what has he caused to be that artefact? Perhaps we might say that the central panel of the door was caused to be a relief sculpture. It is, of course, still the central door panel. Alternatively we could suppose that out of some shapeless lump of clay, or out of sand, cement and water, someone makes a sculpture in the round. There seems to creep into accounts of these latter sorts of processes a suggestion that in doing these things the maker's art "transforms" something, the shapeless materials, into something else. I think we are less tempted to say these things of the former sorts of cases. Yet there surely should be no very great logical difference between cases of making something where, as it were, the materials are "used up" in the process and those cases where the materials are used by being inscribed or decorated yet otherwise still remain the things they are. Perhaps the word "transform" is merely a bit of dramatic licence. But it can still have misleading suggestions.

We should not draw philosophical conclusions from the mere feeling that there is something magical about how a sculptor plys his trade: or at least if we do mean that a sculptor does magically transform one thing into another, we should know what we mean. Magical transformations are common enough in fairy stories. There are good reasons why they should stay there. When the Bad Witch turns the Prince into a frog that is a magical transformation all right. What was once the Prince is now, poor fellow, a frog on the lady's pillow. There he is lying there trying to convince her that he really does love her, really is a handsome prince, while all he can do is stretch himself to his full four inches and croak. But then, his predicament is that he is really a handsome prince in all but appearance: it is a terrible predicament just because, having been changed in appearance, it is quite possible that she will never realise what he really is and kiss his ugly face to change him back to looking right for a prince of his sort.

Of course the Witch might have done something worse still. She might have made a frog, a perfectly ordinary frog, out of the Prince in much the same way that little boys are made out of slugs and snails and puppy dogs' tails, maybe by using him up and boiling him down in the process. Then, of course, there would really *not* be a prince on the Princess's pillow. But then that would not be the same sort of transformation at all, and it still would not even if the Princess found that she had the strange ability to make handsome princes by taking frogs to bed with her and kissing them. It would make no difference to the situation whether the Witch achieves her wicked ways by long boilings of prince's parts in her kitchen or by the simple wave of a magic wand: either way it will turn out that the feat that is performed is that of annihilating the Prince and producing a frog. Part of the fascination of stories of magical transformations is that we don't quite know what it is that has happened: that is part of the magic. There is a sort of shimmer in our imaginative vision between two different sorts of stories. The shimmer is between a story that we might fit into the schema,

(Ex) (at some earlier time x was a prince, and then at some time later the Bad Witch brought it about that x was a frog)
and

The Bad Witch brought about that, (Ex) (before t x was a prince) and at some time after t (Ey) (y was a frog) and at no time was it the case that x and y existed together.
If the first sort of story really is a story of a transformation then it must at least be true that somehow or other the very same thing that was later on a frog was that which was the Prince and became one again after the Princess's administrations. That is a story about changing something, not about bringing something altogether new into existence: part of the magic of the fairy story is that it can come to look like something else. Outside fairy stories we had best avoid these ambiguities.

Accordingly, if we are to construe the claim that the maker of something really did make it the least we can allow him is that he brought it new into existence—*whatever* he had to do to achieve that. So it will be at the very least misleading (much as the fairy story is) to say that he brought it about that (Ex) (x was an A *and x was made to be A*). One cannot have it both ways inside that bracket. The alternative that is then forced on us is to spell out the statement that a maker of something made it something as follows,

> M brought it about that (Ex) (x was an A, e.g. a statue) and (Ey) (y was changed by M to become f, e.g. a block of stone was carved, polished, etc.)
> and such changes in y were sufficient to bring x into being as an A, and this was known to M and formed an essential part of his intentions, or thought in what he was doing.

In other words, of nothing at all that a maker makes is it the case that *that thing* was made to be the thing he makes. This is not for the reason that while he is making it it is not yet, but because what any maker works on, what a sculptor carves, or a carpenter handles, is his materials, not the finished product. As far as any relation, or lack of a relation of the maker to the final object of his making is concerned making and creating in the special sense of creating *ex nihilo* are in the same logical boat. The process of a maker's activity has to do with his materials: it is a contingent fact that normally such a process is necessary for bringing any new thing made into being. "M made A" never (in the presently relevant sense of "made") reports something that M did to A.

It might be objected that this suggests on the one hand that there really is very little of philosophical interest with respect to the logic of making about the special case of creating, and on the other hand that in any case such a conclusion rides roughshod over what we both say and really do mean about making things. When we say that a writer works on his story, a carpenter finishes and polishes the chair that he is making, a sculptor the piece of sculpture he is working on, don't we mean just what we say, namely that they are doing things to these objects themselves?

This second objection is essentially correct. We do really and rightly mean these things, but therein lies the true philosophical relevance of the special idea of creating *ex nihilo*. This may seem paradoxical, but the point lies in the somewhat vague final clause of the above analysis of the statement that a maker made A, namely that to do with his intention in making what he did.

Geach illustrates his thesis concerning the difference between making and creating by appealing to a difference between two ways in which one may be said to be looking for a detective story. In effect these are on the one hand where there is a specific detective story for which one is looking and on the other where one is looking for a specific detective story. While they differ from one another in *that*, in the latter case it is not, while in the former case it is, a condition of the truth of each of these pairs that the seeker should know very clearly indeed what it is that he is looking for. As we have seen, the idiomatic English expression "I have a particular x in mind for which I am looking" does not have to do with that existential condition but expresses a contrast with a "state of intention" where I am not so particular, where perhaps more or less any old detective story will do. Either of the former pair of statements makes, or gets very near to making, the assumption that there exists a *description of* a possible state of affairs (in this case that state of affairs that is the case when the seeker has found a detective story—and of course he *can* only find a particular detective story) and that the seeker can formulate that description. Then, of course, we can go ahead with Geach's contrast and say that *either* the seeker is attempting to make it the case *that something* answers to that description, or that *of something* it is the case that A is seeking to make it the case that it answers to that description. But that contrast simply fails to express what is meant by the difference between my being, or not being *all that particular about* what it is that I want, still less does it have anything to do with those very familiar cases of seeking for something where, while having a rather general idea of the sort of thing that might satisfy me, I really do not know quite what it is that will do the trick. I may want something to read, but still not know what will not bore me as much as the last thing I tried: in this case I still want something to read—there may even *be* something *that* I want to read, even though I am only clear that I want to read *something*.

We may see the point of this for making things if we consider those cases where one would *not* say of a maker that he was working on the thing he is making, as opposed to working at making it. We would not, for example, say this about a man stamping washers on an assembly line. He is making things right enough, and working hard at it, handling, altering and changing materials, but it is the sheet metal he is doing things to and with, not the washers: once they drop into the hopper they are, as far as he is concerned, finished and done with. In general, we would not talk of a maker *working on* what he makes in any case of that sort of highly regulated work where there is no place for doubt or hesitation concerning how the final product is to be. Sometimes, to be sure, the process of making may go wrong—bent pieces of metal may come out of the machine instead of washers, or they may not fit the specification, but then they are rejected as failures: the specification precedes the job.

Of course this is not so in the case of a sculptor working on his sculpture, and is often not so in the case of a carpenter working freely (often but not necessarily by hand) on a piece of woodwork: we can talk of the maker working on what he is making in these cases precisely because they involve to a greater or lesser degree an element of discovery about what it is that will count for the maker as the finished artefact. The logical gap between acting on materials and doing something to what is made is only sharp and clear when the specification of what is to be made more or less completely precedes the making of it. Popularly, we are often inclined to call such methods of making less "creative" than any others. A man stamping washers is popularly, and to a very large extent rightly, regarded as doing the paradigmaticly least "creative", and most boring and soulless job imaginable. Naturally enough in any case where for some reason or other (perhaps a theological one) we wish to say that the making involves no materials, there can be no possible area of overlap between a report of the process of the agent's making and a report of his succeeding in making something. This leaves us with the rather fine irony that the closest analogy we can find to divine creation in the workaday world is the most uncreative of work. Only there is it clearly the case that the report that M made A unambiguously rules out M doing something to A.

This certainly gives us the end of a scale, but a scale *within* the context of ordinary making. A highly perfectionist craftsman, used to success and very clear about how he wants the object he is making to be completed, will, no more than the stamper of washers, report that he is still working *on* that object, his report will be, or the sense of it will be, that he is working *towards* it. At the other end of the scale we can imagine the child making sand castles, or Tommy making his clown at school. As they proceed objects "emerge" from the changes they make in the materials, to be recognised and accepted as possible candidates for being counted as the individuals being made: that they emerge from a semi chaos does not mean that the children are merely making messes. No thing emerges from chaos if it is just a mess one is making.

Of course this end of the scale can have its theological echoes too, though less scholastic ones. Paul Klee, in describing this process of discovery of what it is that one is making in the process of making it, also makes a specific reference to divine creativity; "shortly after the first movement the first counter movement sets in . . . In plain English: the creator looks to see what he has achieved so far (and, says the Bible, it was good)."[3]

The two ends of the scale here have tended to produce quite traditional, and often opposed, conceptions of the place of thought in action. That there tends to be such an opposition is one of the reasons for the neglect of much serious exploration of the forms of thought that may be involved in the action of making things. Accordingly, it may be well to look closer at some prevalent accounts of thinking and acting with this in mind.

Notes

1 *God and the Soul,* Routledge, 1969, pp. 82–3.
2 A. N. Prior, *Papers on Time and Tense.* Oxford University Press 1967. pp. 73–4.
3 Paul Klee, *The Thinking Eye,* Lund Humphreys, 1961, p. 357.

CHAPTER TWO

THOUGHT IN ACTION AND THOUGHT ABOUT ACTION

THE theological opposition which I have touched on in the previous chapter between a conception of a maker's activity that opens a logical gap between acting on materials and doing something to what is made and a conception of a maker's activity where there is no such gap might be labelled, if we choose to adopt somewhat traditional theological or metaphysical teminology, as that between a picture of a creator who is "transcendental" to his creation and one where his process of thought (perhaps God's "shaping spirit") is "imminant" in the process of his creation's coming to be. What I am suggesting therefore is that very much this kind of contrast (perhaps not quite the same, since the technical terminology of metaphysics or theology naturally develops its own somewhat rarefied sophistication) reappears in that between the sort of maker's activity exemplified by a worker on an assembly line and that of a sculptor "working on" his materials. It is not a central part of my purpose to explore these theological matters, but they may be worth bearing in mind if only to remind us how our attitudes to the activities of makers of things can be deeply rooted both in quite traditional metaphysics and at the same time in our more familiar descriptions of what people do and of the conditions under which they do them.

It is an everyday commonplace that the situation of an assembly line worker engaged in the activity of providing the stereotyped means to a predetermined end is engaged in an activity that must quite obviously contrast with free "creative" work, and one which, moreover, may involve a degree of tedium that cries to Heaven, or perhaps to Revolution, for justice. What is by no means so obvious, however, is what it is that this contrast amounts to. It can be, for instance, sometimes too easily, sentimentally, supposed that his predicament might be resolved by the political act of freeing him from being the mere agent of the externally imposed plans and policies of that boss to whom he has sold his labour. But, of course, even if he were himself the owner and master of the process he is engaged in, making washers for himself, for his fellows or the community of which he was a participating member, it is not clear that to that extent the activity of making that he is engaged in would of itself be any different. He might conceivably feel happier about performing it, but that would be another matter, for if we are concerned with the nature of a certain activity of bringing something into being it is to the nature of the agent's thought, or lack of it, *in* that activity, as opposed to his thought *about* it that we should pay attention rather than to its external circumstances.

My use of this distinction may well seem obscure, but it is, I believe, quite fundamental, and I also believe often quite disastrously overlooked, often by being obscured among other distinctions. It may be as well therefore to begin with some attempt to illustrate this.

It is a truism that thought may manifest itself as much in what people do as in what they say. This truism can easily seem to transform itself into a rather more profound philosophical truth by the seemingly innocent device of inventing a pair of abstract entities called "theoretical thinking" and "practical thinking" and distinguishing between the two by holding that the former expresses itself in language and the latter in action. The effect of this way of putting the matter is to suggest that there are not only two ways in which people may act on what they think but also two different ways of thinking. It is equally truistic that some *arguments* may be concerned with what is the case and others with what ought to be the case. Since doing is (equally truistically) a practical matter, it can thus easily seem to be a straightforward matter of relabelling to call these latter sorts of arguments practical arguments while the others, since the term provides a natural contrast, are theoretical ones. In this way these several truisms can be innocently run together so that it can seem that we have to do with a single division that can be variously called that between what is theoretical and what is practical, or alternatively, between asserting, or saying, something as the outcome of thought and doing something, or again between arguing that something is the case and arguing that something ought to be the case. The terminology of philosophical discussions, perhaps most insidiously, the labelling of philosophical courses, has a tendency to run through this gamut of distinctions with a quite remarkable indifference. Some of the intellectual embarrassment that this can give rise to might be well illustrated by noting some of the reactions philosophers may have to what can be regarded as the first (literally classical) discussion in this area which is what Aristotle said about what he called, or is called by his translators, the "practical syllogism".

In the *Nicomachean Ethics* Aristotle made a distinction, which has provided a peg for countless subsequent philosophical comments and commentaries which at one point he marked very simply by saying that whereas in the case of the "theoretical syllogism" "the mind is forced to *affirm* the conclusion, so in the practical syllogism we are straightway forced to do it".[1] If we take this statement literally it certainly does not seem to have to do with a distinction between practical arguments which issue in a statement, a conclusion, that something ought to be the case, or with a stated injunction to some agent that he should do something or other, as opposed to "theoretical" arguments that issue in a stated conclusion that something or other is the case, for even if something of that sort of distinction is just around the corner, or was at the back of Aristotle's mind, it cannot be expressed in this way. For someone to state that something should be the case, or to enjoin another to do something is at all events to say something, or in rather general terms to "affirm" something, while equally, on the other hand to say or "affirm" something is by the same token to do something, at all events to speak.

Perhaps the letter of what Aristotle may have said does not matter in the least: the point should be what he, a philosopher of manifest pertinacity, must have really meant. Inevitably, of course, different commentators have had altogether different ideas of what the underlying sensible and uncontroversial thoughts of the master must have been. In this case the differences are sharp and clear enough, and they do, it seems to me, exhibit an issue of some considerable philosophical importance and one which is in a peculiar way central to this study of a maker's thought and action.

Alisdair MacIntyre, says for example, of Aristotle's remarks:

> That the conclusion is an action makes it plain that the practical syllogism is a pattern of reasoning by the agent and not a pattern of reasoning by others of what the agent ought to do . . . Nor indeed is it a pattern of reasoning by the agent about what he ought to do. It is not to be confused with perfectly ordinary syllogisms, whose conclusion is a statement of that order. Its whole point is to probe the sense in which an action may be the outcome of reasoning.[2]

Clearly, on this account there is seen to be nothing at all wrong with the idea that an action *itself* may be the "conclusion" of an argument and moreover the implication of MacIntyre's comments must be that for anyone to deny this is for him at the same time to deny that there can be a radical distinction between the thought of an agent for himself in acting and the thought of himself, or of others about what he ought to do. One may judge for others, tell others what to do, but one can only perform one's own actions. The underlying suggestion seems to be that whereas judgement *about* an action (one's own or another's) is general, actions are particular. But, it may be objected, so long as the action is the outcome of *thought* and so long as in any sense we can suppose that that thought is tantamount to the thought that that action should be performed—and it may be hard to see how there could be any relevant account of the thought concerned that does not involve this—it is that that is central to the story, and *that*, it may be urged, is a reason for acting that the agent in acting is aware of.

Now, if we pursue this line of thinking, it must be clear that a reason for acting, in any sense in which it can be the conclusion of an argument (or a syllogism, if we stick to the language of the debate) must be so in just the same sense in which something or other might be the premise of the argument but in *that* sense the very idea of action *itself* being the conclusion of an argument is quite absurd. To be sure one might well conclude, or finish, arguing, or having an argument, by doing something or other, but then that is then just not the sense either of "conclusion" or of "argument" that should be in question. One may begin an argument by doing something too, but then what one is doing is not the argument's premise, for what one does is not a proposition, and it is only in the sense in which a conclusion is a proposition that logically follows from its premises that an argument which is a rational pattern of thought can have a "conclusion".[3]

Where does this leave us? On the face of it, if we stick to the letter of my quotation from Aristotle, it would seem to involve a quite silly mistake, the mistake equivalent to confusing two quite different senses of the phrase "a conclusion of an argument". How are we to "probe the sense in which an action may be the outcome of reasoning"? Is there one at all?

To make matters worse the Aristotelian remark is perhaps even more puzzling in another way when it seems to claim that in the case of a practical syllogism the agent is "straightway forced" to do what he does. Forced, we might ask, how and in what sense? It may make fairly clear sense to say that the premises of an argument "force" a certain conclusion, that is to say that they logically "compel" i.e. imply that conclusion, but it is hard to see how some proposition, or collection of propositions could force or compel anyone to do anything. It is just as hard to see how the further fact that such a collection of propositions implies another could force anyone to do anything, let alone "straightway". That someone might suppose so would seem to indicate that he had fallen victim to a confusion that is all of a piece with that of failing to distinguish between "conclusion" in the sense in which some proposition might be implied by another —is the logical conclusion of an argument—and the sense in which the activity of arguing might be concluded or finished in some way or another by further confusing the idea of a logical connection—implication—with the idea of a causal connection, of something bringing something about. And this seems to be a very elementary mistake to make.

One reply to this might be that even though it may be clear

enough that logical connections and causal connections are very different things the very fact that people can act on what they think (can be rational in any sense at all) must also show that they may in just these sorts of cases be connected. Indeed it seems obvious enough that the very fact that there can be rational agents at all is the fact of that connection. This connection could be expressed idiomatically by saying that while it is on the one hand clear enough that the "logicians" sense of "argument", in which he may refer to the argument that p implies q, is different enough from that commoner sense of "argument" in which one may complain of being kept awake by the interminable argument going on in the next room, it cannot possibly be an accident that the two words are the same. Of course it is not an accident, for to argue with someone is typically to point out to him that one thing does imply another, and to argue with him about what he ought to do is similarly to point out to him that he ought to do something or other is implied by something else. If he believes that (the premise) then he must—one is urging by argument—also accept that he should act so. In much the same way one may argue with oneself, or, more idiomatically, one may reason and to reason *is* to reflect on reasons for things and the root of *that* idea must be that a reason for q is p just when p logically implies q. In this way reason can be both practical and theoretical for the very good "reason" that it is a matter of complete indifference whether "q" has to do with what is the case or what ought to be the case.[4]

The upshot of this reply would then be to say that there is a possible, if misleadingly expressed, way in which one may "straightway" act on the conclusion of a practical argument. That sense would be one we could less misleadingly express by saying that having reached certain conclusions concerning what we ought to do, we may act on them straightaway, there being no further relevant considerations.

However, while much of this may be true, it may also be felt that somehow such reflections miss the point. They do so because it infortunately is not the case that people do always act straightway on what they suppose they should do, and sometimes not at all. We might well be tempted to feel that this is a "mere" psychological complication and this is very much the bias of reflections along these lines, for they suggest a philosophical programme in which what we have to consider is not the place of thought in action, but rather the various ways in which certain actions, along with beliefs, may be justified. If it is felt that these are different questions that feeling is tantamount to a suspicion that these are not "merely psychological" complications.

I might well infer from hearing my alarm clock sounding in my ear that it is time for me to get up, but there I lie indolently contemplating the conclusions of my inferences. Nothing at all forces me out of bed, certainly not straightaway, and neither does anything force me to "affirm" (say) that I should do so. Of course I know that I should, may have thought out why I should, may even tell myself to do so, but still I do not leave my bed. Hume's well-known doctrine that reason is altogether inert to initiate action seems manifestly correct just before breakfast, for then nothing is more obvious than that *I* am inert. Perhaps Aristotle was an early riser?

On the other hand, perhaps not, for it is very largely in the context of considering situations in someways not unlike this that he introduced this very topic into the history of philosophy. A general name he seems to have reserved for the sort of agent whose actions do not connect with his thoughts in this and in other sorts of ways is that which is rather unfortunately translated into English as the "incontinent man". This is unfortunate enough if it suggests to the reader that the standard example of this sort of thing is a failure to leap out of bed in response to reflections concerning the imminent consequences of an uncomfortable bladder, but it is doubly unfortunate when, rather more solemnly, the topic is seen as having to do with what is generally called "weakness of will", and sometimes seen as having to do with insincerity.

Clearly enough, of course, a slugabed is as standard a case of a weak will as we are likely to find, if not always an extreme one, and equally clearly there is *something* insincere about one who concludes that he ought to get up and does not, though only *something* for the case would not even be intelligible if he did not really think that he ought to do what he is failing to do, but we should be careful not to jump to conclusions on the basis of just one sort of case. Aristotle himself offers a remarkably wide list of cases, and it is a list which should give us pause for thought and which can lead us back to the case of the bored worker on the assembly line. The idea of incontinence, or of weak will may initially suggest to us a picture of idle slobs, of drunks, those who may be in the grip of rage or swept off their feet by lust ("it was an irresistible impulse M'Lud") but, while he may have had cases of this sort in mind too, some of his examples are surprisingly different. "People," he says "suffering from the sort of disabilities I have mentioned will repeat to you the proof of some problem in geometry or a passage from Empedocles". He means without understanding what they are talking about. "In the same way people who have begun the study of a subject reel off a string of propositions which they do not as yet understand. For knowledge must be worked into the living texture of the mind, and this takes time. So we should think of incontinent men as like actors—mouthpieces for the sentiments of other people."[5]

This is insincerity and weakness of will all right, but insincerity seen in a different light. For these last examples are of those who say what they do not mean: the impression one gets from the drift of Aristotle's examples is that such people are in the same case as those who do what they do not mean, or do not do what they do mean. I do not mean that they are in the same situation as those who do, or do not do, what they do not, or do, mean *to do*. It is not a matter of intention in quite that sense. It is as if we have to place novices at a skill or craft in the same category as those who are "drunk or in the grip of rage", but the clue is provided if we think of the sort of party drunk who is not raging or out cold but who rambles on about *Finegan's Wake* and the Uncertainty Principle without the least idea what he has in mind, or who absent-mindedly makes love to his own wife in mistake for someone else's. In none of these cases is there a clear answer to the question "what was his thought in what he did?". We do not have a general word for the opposite of absence of mind (it is certainly not presence of mind) but the word, where we do have it would have to do with what it is for *either* speech *or* action to be an expression of thought. And that idea is not simply that of such things being *justified*. How might we show the need for this?

Suppose we are tempted to suppose that to say that an agent's action "straightway" follows his thought means, if it means anything at all merely that some proposition concerning what should be done is both accepted by the agent and "directly" follows from certain premises that he also accepts. In this light we might give as a biographical fragment for an agent's concluding that he should act according to certain principles,

Believing that [people should be kind to philosophers]
and believing that [the person he was dealing with was a philosopher]
he concluded that [he should be kind to that person]

or, in the case where the agent's thought is concerned with doing something as a means to a certain end,

Believing that [X was a good thing to seek (or, more simply, if slightly differently, wanting X)]
and believing that [Y was the best means to X]
he concluded that [he should do (or bring about) Y.]

Such a way of construing the agent's biography has the apparent advantage that the verbs of mental action ("believing", "concluding", etc.) can be split off from the expressions in square brackets with the result that we are presented with a picture of the agent's running through an argument of the appropriate logical form in such a way that our concern for their "logic" can be seen as a quite separate thing from our concern for his mental activity (which we can see then as another "psychological" matter). That the conclusions whatever they are follow from their premises is then clearly a different matter from the fact that the agent concluded whatever he did. And in one way it clearly is.

But if we are to give any sort of an account of the agent's biography in these cases that relevantly relates to his thought in what he did—actually gives us an intellectual biography of his actions—we shall need a further crucial addition. We shall need to add that what he concluded that he should do he actually did do, for of course, he very well might not have done. We need to add, "So that's what he did". In just the same way if someone concludes that something or other is the case we shall need to add, if it is true, as it might well not be, "So that's what he said". But, then what is the force of the "so" here?

An obvious answer is that the force of the "so" is that it explains why the agent acted or spoke as he did—because he thought in a certain way. But why does it explain this? Are we to suppose that the agent was caused to act or speak so? But then, he might not have, so perhaps in those cases we should look for some events of processes that interrupt that causal process. It certainly cannot be that it logically follows that he spoke or acted thus so should we conclude that the agent (in common with all other agents whatsoever) has a practical, perhaps even an ethical, principle that he should act how he thinks he should or speak what he thinks is so? But, despite any other attractions or advantages (for it may be that there is some sense in which rational agents do have a principle to say what they think is so in default of good reasons not to) it should be clear enough that such a view merely involves a regress, for we then have the question of the agent acting on *that* principle . . . and so on.

In default of any other answer it seems that we must fall back on something like the causal answer, but it seems to be a slightly queer sort of causation—we might call it the causality of thought (to call it psychological causation seems to be misleading). This is perhaps one of the underlying reasons why philosophers have sometimes been tempted to call the principles of logic the laws of thought, since they do at least show us where it is that such causality comes into play. A feature of such causality is that it is characteristically inhibitions to clear thinking such as being embarrassed, distracted, confused, frightened, (along with being drunk or drugged, if one will, but these things are not the most common factors) that can interrupt the process. But most centrally of all will be a simple, if radical form of incompetence. One may be verbally incompetent, just bad at putting what one thinks into words, and this has its parallel in non-verbal action. Verbal incompetence has its parallel in kack-handedness. Philosophers have on the whole neglected the central place of this fascinating phenomenon in the philosophy of action.

It should be noted how very strange it is that otherwise intelligent and physically able people can find themselves unable to follow perfectly simple instructions (which they understand well enough in the sense that they may be able to repeat or translate them to others) for changing a simple fuse or a typewriter ribbon. Where saying and doing parallel one another the common notion for each can be "expression". To be kack-handed, or tongue-tied is not to be able to express thought in doing or saying. Abilities here can be disparate. Just as one may not be able to act on a piece of practical knowledge that he can readily put into words, so another may not be able to say what it is that he knows perfectly well how to do.

It is a philosophical commonplace that in the case of verbal expression one certainly does not need to run through the silent conclusion that one ought to say something or other as a preliminary to acting on it—one "straightway speaks". One does not need to, but one might. Sometimes, if one is out of ease with the company, shy, embarrassed, speaking in a foreign language, and so on, one may have to. For there one's ability to speak as one thinks is not "worked into the living texture of the mind". There seems no reason whatsoever to suppose that the situation is in any way different in the case of action. When one is not, distracted, not embarrassed, not shy, overtired (sometimes in the Parliamentary sense) one may act as one thinks, "straightaway" as the conclusion, the direct outcome, of thought.

A quite different piece of thought-in-action is reported by saying of someone that "he concluded that he should Ø, and accordingly did so" from that described (having reported the premises in the same way) by saying more simply" . . . so he did Ø". To make the conclusions of practical arguments inevitably the performance of some mental act (he concluded that *p*) is to obscure that difference. To a significant extent this difference can be seen primarily exhibited in the difference between the characteristic behaviour of a practical expert and that of an apprentice or an amateur. We could suppose an experienced craftsman making a cupboard and cutting a mortice joint for it. His knowledge and experience has taught him that a certain sort of chisel is right for the job (is "fitting" to use an expression that seems to have been close to Aristotle's). Knowing this and recognising the appropriate chisel before him on the bench, he uses it. His action of using the right thing in the right way at the right time *is* what constitutes his thought in what he does. This is no different from the case where a fluent speaker's use of the right words in the right order is what constitutes his thought in speaking. One acts his mind, the other speaks it. One means what he does, the other in just the same sense says what he means.

Suppose such a practical agent is interrupted and asked why it is that he does what he does, why he uses his tools in that particular way. Then, he may pause and explain, but then he is searching for words, not attending to his actions with tools and wood, and because the direction of his attention is different his actions and his thought in what he does are different: he is then teaching, explaining, instructing, not carpentering. (The key word here is "attention", not "intention"). Certainly, it is crucial that, if his teaching is to be honest, what he tells the apprentice must be the verbal analogue of his thought in what he does when carpentering. It is equally crucial that we should not conclude from this that his thought in what he does must be a matter of some inner, silent, process that accompanies, or precedes his actions, nor that we should look for some ghostly version of such a verbal train in his believing and concluding.

On the other hand in the case of the apprentice *that* may be just what we *should* look for and just what we may find (or find in ourselves by introspection) for he very likely will formulate just those propositions and conclusions *about* what he should do that amount to his running through in his mind the practical *theory* of the relevant actions—a theory taught him by his instructors. It is familiar enough in experience that because he has to attend to that—to what he thinks, or remembers that he ought to do—he is in no position to attend fully to what he is doing.

It might be objected to this that while there may be some reason for connecting the various ideas of meaning what one says and doing what one means, there are still more obvious and better reasons for making distinctions here, for it must be obvious enough, for instance, that that sense in which a word may have a "meaning" is completely different from any sense in which someone may mean to do whatever it is he does. I would not wish to deny this for a minute. But in bearing such denials in mind, we should not at the same time forget what it is that may connect these various, and often quite different idea. As I have already hinted, one way of getting at the connections can be via the idea of successful expression. It is significant, and in many ways regrettable, that this is an idea that is often almost exclusively associated with the notion of successful expression in the arts, rather as if artists alone might, in any philosophically interesting way be supposed to express themselves in what they make or do. This is, of course, quite absurd. The idea of successful expression is a perfectly general one which we might, perhaps rather baldly, put as follows.

If someone means what he says (has expressed himself successfully) then the correct and only answer we can give to the question what it was that he meant is to repeat what he said, or something that we can accept as synonymous with what he said. Similarly if someone does what he means to do then what it was that he meant to do can equally only be either what he did or something that we, and he, can accept as equivalent to it. These rather truistic observations can lead to a less truistic consequence, for they can put us on our guard against a temptation to say that in the case where someone says what he means some further thing "what he means" (his meaning, or his thought, even his intention) has a special relation—that of being expressed in—what he says, and a similar and quite parallel temptation to say that in the case where someone does what he means "what he means" (his "practical thought", his intention) may have a similar special relation to what he does. But it should be clear that this temptation (which has often given rise to a whole host of philosophical red herrings, including much discussion in Aesthetics of the folly of trying to judge a work by the artist's intentions) need have no hold on us at all. For what such a way of thinking overlooks is what ought to be the rather obvious fact that it is only in those cases of *unsuccessful* expression, where one does not manage to say what one means, or do what one means, or where one has not *yet* said or done what one means to, that it is necessary to look beyond what was said or done. One may envisage what one wants to say or do, one may imagine or seek to formulate in one's mind what one might, or should have, said or done if only one *had* been successful, and in such cases of course it is true that an intelligent, rational, agent thinks *about* his actions, or his possible actions, but in all other cases there is no such gap to open up between an agent's thought and his action: in such successful cases it is the agent's actions themselves that are the expression of his thought.

There is a dominant tradition in the philosophy of action, a pervasive tone of voice, that seems to wish to deny this, that sees the whole topic of thought and action, of "practical reason", as being about thought about action, about what actions we might, or should, or should have performed. Running through that tradition is a certain picture of rational activity, where the agent asks himself what it is that he wants, what his goals are, what it is that he intends to do, then having asked himself, or being told by others, what will bring about that end, acts accordingly, or where he, having certain general principles, concerning what sorts of things should be done, then seeks to perform those actions that will conform to those principles. Well, of course, intelligent agents, rational men, do think and act in this way, but to see this as the whole picture is to connive at a significant distortion. For it is no accident that this is the language of justification, the bias of those who are professionally or by inclination teachers or administrators, whose business it is to stand outside the actions of themselves and others and to legislate for them. This is a bias that looks to be suspiciously ideological, that which sees practical intelligence as the province of those that know what should be done and why. Philosophers have perhaps long since abandoned the exciting ambition of being philosopher kings; they restrict themselves to the more attainable ideal of being philosopher vice chancellors.

Perhaps we should not talk too glibly about ideologies in this context. It may be that the most that we can say—which should be enough in all conscience—is that there may be certain tenacious and widespread attitudes, that inform a rather general tradition of thought. But then, if that tradition of thought can at the same time be related, however generally, to a pattern of social attitudes, for instance to a movement for social reform, that may be just what in the most general sense we should take an ideology to be. It can be a mistake to suppose that we *can* do much more in this sort of area than talk in generalities, for some truths may just be general, even vague, and be none the worse for that.

In this vein we might take a passing look at the movement of enlightened social reform, liberal, utilitarian, that socialists from the nineteenth century onwards (not only Marx and Marxists) have seen in more or less specific terms as representing a bourgeois ideology. Very generally, the charge against that tradition amounts to saying that despite the undoubted benefits liberal reformers conferred in combatting arbitrary and superstitious power they still saw themselves as being those very people most capable of being the enlightened administrators of the reformed society. Thus, since they were for the most part already (albeit critical) members of the governing classes their very radicalism amounted to a form of conservative retrenchment. Despite their undoubted insistence on the paramount value of freedom, such freedom inevitably tends to be circumscribed by the, not always tacit, proviso that it should only be exercised within the framework of a system of law and a social order which they themselves could administer. Briefly, from many points of view unfairly, though this is just the sort of unfairness which may be perceived differently from different points of view, the *moral* implications of the charge are that such reformers are guilty of that infuriating form of elitist snobbery of those who seek to do good for the generality of mankind regardless of whether the subjects of their reforms know what is good for them or not. It is significant that a feeling of frustrated anger at such attitudes may as commonly be expressed from the populist right as from the left.

In many ways, of course, such a view *is* unfair. The idea that there should be a specifically enlightened sort of good man whose clear thinking and virtuous understanding gave him a right to govern others is at least as old as Plato's *Republic* and at all events Plato's version of it would be bound to be repudiated by a liberal utilitarian such as J. S. Mill for whom it was essential that social wisdom could not be derived from anything remotely like the contemplation of the form of the Good by those of the finest nature, but in the open and egalitarian forum of rational debate. Still, however, an embarrassment can remain that has at least something to do with a characteristic inability of those within the tradition of liberal enlightenment to see how the charges made against it could be anything *else* than quite unfair. Their rationalist conscience which is all of a piece with their conscientious sense of rationality remains quite amazingly untroubled by such attacks.

We can find some clues to why this is in Mill himself. In a famous passage in *Utilitarianism*[6] where he is arguing why there should be an over-riding principle in any rational morality, he says "there ought to be some one fundamental principle or law at the root of all morality, or, if there be several, there should be a determinate order of precedence among them; and the one principle, or the rule for deciding between the various principles should be self-evident". Elsewhere he refers to the need for some standard by which to determine the goodness or badness, absolute or comparative of ends or objects of desire and in general Mill saw the very idea of one ultimate over-riding principle indifferently as an ultimate end. The principle of utility, to seek to promote the greatest happiness of the greatest number seems on the face of it to be a goal to which all rational men's actions should be directed. Now, it may be true that there is no need to regard the greatest happiness of the greatest number as some ultimate goal to be realised in an ideal social state (as opposed to happiness being the concept for a general principle for evaluating any goal) and it may well be that Mill did not so conceive the idea;[7] what is significant is that his way of using the terms of his argument should have made readers suppose that it should be on this sort of point they should take issue with him. This, together with the extraordinary picture of a sort of rational optimism that supposes that (even in some ideal state of affairs) all moral and political conflicts could finally be resolved within the framework of an over-riding system is the immediate picture that seems to be presented to the reader's attention by his style of argument. In fact the two things are fairly directly connected.

If all choices can be seen as being able to be brought under one head as leading to some single further type of state then only one preference need stand apart from the possibility of rational justification, namely the preference for that type of state. If that preference is self-evident so much the better for our general account of rational justification of actions. Whether we think of that self-evident preference as a preference for a final state or a single self-evident principle for opting for a variety of situations the underlying picture will still be the same, namely that we have a single rational system in which we can seek to justify any action in terms of what it may lead to.

But, of course, to justify an action in terms of its falling under a principle for right action is a different thing altogether from justifying it as tending to promote a desired end. For example to give as a reason for doing something that it was the right sort of thing to do in the circumstances is not, or not necessarily to be concerned with the action itself being a means to a certain end. If knowing that a polite remark is called for one asks after the health of someone's wife one need not be (though of course one might be) seeking to achieve anything by doing so, and if, dimly suspecting that one ought to pass the port in one direction rather than another one muffs the whole business and knocks the stuff over one has not thereby failed to achieve some *goal* by adopting incorrect means. Competently, or incompetently one has simply managed, or failed to do the right thing; to do something or other because it was the right thing to do in the circumstances, or even the right thing to do in any circumstances, is normally and rightly contrasted with doing something to achieve something further. There may be many reasons that we may have for doing something that are not means-ends reasons; one such is "for its own sake", another is because it is fitting, the right thing to do, or "on principle".

Yet a picture of all actions being "ideally" justifiable in that they can lead to some ultimate sort of state can easily seem to be of a piece with a picture of an ideally rational world of human action where the justification for performing any particular action can be placed in an ordered hierarchy of principles for action. Certain confusions can help this process along, for sometimes the verbal expression for these two sorts of consideration can look very alike. For instance, to say "If you want to be really rude to James tell him his ears stick out when he next tries to discuss philosophy with you" can seem to be a merely idiomatic variant on saying "if you want to offend and infuriate James tell him that his ears stick out when he next tries to discuss philosophy with you" and they each seem to suggest some hypothetical goal to which such outrageous behaviour is a possible means. But in fact being rude to James *is* what is outrageous about that behaviour whereas upsetting and insulting him is what might be achieved by being so rude to him (of course he might be so good natured, or deaf, that even that rudeness failed). But in this general context we are dealing with something that cuts deeper.

That one thing may lead to another and that we can know that it can is what we must finally rely on if we are to decide to do, or justify doing, anything in means-end terms. Moreover, just as little drops of water and little grains of sand may make a mighty ocean and a pleasant land, so can little deeds of kindness and the rest lead to a heaven, if not above, at all events on earth. How can we know that such small and insignificant actions can be made to be part of such a grand design? Obviously by knowing how it is that one thing can lead to another, by having in our possession a body of scientific knowledge. And it is in terms of such rational optimism that scientific principles and practical principles can seem to bear a close analogy to each other—or would do so if we knew what we needed to know. In its simplest form the relation that a particular action has to a principle governing it is that of a species being included in a genus. The argument that justifies an action on principle is that actions of a certain kind are called for in certain situations, these particular actions and situations are of that kind, hence they should be performed in those circumstances. The classificatory class inclusion pattern can clearly be carried on in the other direction with genera of a lower kind being included in progressively higher genera and in this way it can be easy enough to imagine a picture of a total deductive system in which the justifiability of any action can be shown by inferring a hierarchy of progressively more exactly specified actions from more general principles; the ideal is then of making any justification for action conform to this simple deductive pattern. There seems to be no doubt that this picture of rationality in human affairs influenced Mill's thinking and perhaps dominated it.[8]

There is equally no doubt that very much this picture and the ideas associated with it lies behind the main stream of rationally optimistic reforming nineteenth century thinking. Its characteristic is to parallel practical thinking exactly with similarly deductivist accounts of causal explanation in the sciences where progressively more general laws would in an ideal scientific situation be subsumed under progressively more all-embracing covering laws of material causation. Just as we can rationally explain the behaviour of matter in this latter way, so we can explain the behaviour of a truly rational agent along the same lines: the only difference between the two cases can then be that in the former situation we bring our explanatory principles to closer conformity to how things are as our wisdom increases, whereas in our wise and rational action we bring what we do into closer and closer conformity to a system of principles. The upshot of such a picture is that just as a failure to conform to the principles of causal explanation that we have makes the natural world inexplicable, so a refusal to act in conformity with some hierarchy of principles makes an agent's behaviour inexplicable, irrational or non-rational.

It can seem obvious enough that numbers of people do not come into line in this way. Some we can dismiss as confused, irrational and in this sense acceptable among those whose actions are not capable of rational explanation. But some we cannot dismiss so lightly. There are artists, poets, creative writers, people of a certain kind of anarchic sensibility who not only will not fall into line, but who will not for the most serious of reasons. A feeling that this is so—often no more than an angry and confused "romantic" response to the felt threat of what is sometimes referred to as a "rationalist Benthamite world" which somehow excludes what should be held dear—certainly needs explaining and examining in some detail before we can make a very great deal of it, and to a considerable extent it is this examination which is the implicit topic of the later chapters of this book. But meanwhile we should notice something that may be nearer at hand, and which in certain respects can cut deeper.

This is that if we see rational explanation and rational action in these closely parallel terms it can seem obvious that just as a scientific theory is just as true (or false) whoever holds it, or whoever finds it out so a rational system of morals or politics will similarly be just as true (or false) whoever knows it or comes to find it out. Moreover, just as there is an obvious logical distinct-tion between an event and its explanation, so there would by analogy seem to be a similar distinction between an action and its justification. On such an account we will not only not need to draw any philosophically important distinctions between an agent's thought about what he does and his thought in what he does, we had better not do so, for that distinction can seem to be an irrelevant distraction from the central question of the agent's justification for what he does.

If we are inclined to make a wholesale gap between the process of thought that has to do with an action and the action itself, there would seem to be no particular reason whey we should not go the whole hog and let the thinking out and understanding of the relevant practical principles be the business of one set of people while the more lowly matter of putting such principles into practice the job of others. For, if an action has passed muster in terms of whether its performance can be justified according to certain acceptable and commonly accepted as-sumptions, we can obviously regard it as justified for anyone who accepts these principles and assumptions. It can then be rather hard to see why it could ever be that we might feel the least unease about the predicament of a man engaged in the boring but necessary work of stamping out washers on an assembly line. Perhaps he should even feel grateful to us that he has been spared the tedium of working out just why his activities are worth engaging in. Let us suppose, as we well might, that the maker of washers can be persuaded fairly readily that what he is making are good things to have. They can be shown to him to be an essential means to a desired end (one which he desires too, motor cars, maybe). Since he is in no way stupid he can be shown further that what he is doing is the best, or perhaps the only, way of achieving that end. His actions may even further other ends that he accepts as well, so what he is doing can be justified further (even to him). If what he is going is justified, is reasonable, even right, and has, moreover, been justified already before he even sets out to work, why should he complain that he exercises no thought in what he does, for the thought has already been done by others for him?

It is hard to see how an account of rationality that places the idea of reason on the back of that of reasons for actions and thus sees the most rational agent as the best justifier, the best legislator, could fail to reach such elitist conclusions. In a presidential address to the Aristotelian Society Professor Hare has, quite without irony, spelt them out for us suggesting not only that there should be recognised "guardians" who are able to "propound a body of fairly simple and teachable principles which can be used in our actual lives" but that it is "dangerous to question the principles too readily" that "those who have not the time, or lack the ability to do this kind of thinking will be well advised to abide by the principles of those who have done it".[9] This is the authentic voice of the Superior Rational Man, the voice of the theorist of action as opposed to one whose thought finds its expression in action itself, what Eldridge Cleaver in another context,[10] called the Omnipotent Administrator, the voice of the mandarin that finds its natural complement in the predicament of the maker whose actions have been reduced to the merely mechanical, who also expresses no thought in his actions, because his thought has been done for him by others.

This frightening picture of a society divided in this way is, of course partly, if not wholly, satirical. It is our great good fortune that certain philosophical tendencies in our thinking about practical intelligence are never quite overwhelming. The satire would not be complete, however, without adding to it a third component. Set against this pair of opposed social roles is a specially privileged, if mysterious, sort of person, the artist. He, mysteriously and impressively—at least to those who value their own cultural sensibility—can express himself in what he does. His thought does express itself in action, in the action of making things or performing works and above all he is creative.

What I shall be concerned to argue in what follows is, put in the most general terms, this. We have embedded within our attitudes to the nature of rational action, or of intelligent agency, a picture of creativity—most particularly of the creativity of artists—that makes that phenomenon essentially mysterious, a matter "beyond reason" and at the same time special, not a matter for ordinary everyday activity. This is not, I believe, because we put a high value on the place of the arts—the truth is rather the reverse—but because we have a conception of rationality that puts such things out of bounds, literally beyond the bounds of intelligibility. If we are to understand ourselves and others we will need, therefore, to go beyond those boundaries and bring our understanding of an artist's activities back within the area of ordinary experience. To attempt this I shall consider the topic of making in the arts in some detail, but my ultimate purpose is not to do aesthetics. It is in the hope that we may come to see that the characteristic activities of artists are not those of artists alone.

The order of how this might be tackled might be best set out by considering from another point of view the so-called "practical syllogism" with which this chapter is ostensibly concerned. For the idea of the "practical syllogism" (which seems to be no more than that of there being practical arguments) has been, perhaps superficially, misleading by tending to suggest, on the analogy with the traditional Aristotelian "theoretical" syllogism (e.g. All men are mortal, Socrates is a man, so Socrates is mortal) that it is a practical argument in three steps—for instance on the model of the above example, some general principle of what should be done, a claim that some particular action falls under that general principle, and a conclusion. Much of the topic of this chapter has been concerned with the apparently rather narrow question whether there is any sense in which we ought to take the conclusion to be an action itself or rather a judgement that one ought to act in a certain way, and I have argued that it depends on what sort of agent's thought in action one has in mind. There are indeed some traditional Aristotelian examples that seem fit this triadic pattern well enough, for instance the notoriously weird case of reasoning that goes "Dry food is good for the health; this is dry food, so . . . ('eat this', or maybe the agent eats it)". However, many people tend to see a standard form of such arguments, and the tendency starts at least at the beginning of the story with Aristotle himself, as having to do with not general principles and particular cases, but with considerations of means to a certain end. And indeed it really does seem to be the case that that characteristic virtue of being an intelligent agent that corresponds to what Aristotle called "prudence" must at least involve the ability to calculate and to reflect on how to bring what one wants about, as well as the ability for foresee and to evaluate the consequences of ones actions. It is here, however, that an inclination to see a naturally and simple triadic form of argument can be quite misleading.

Such a view can be misleading in that it can quite easily encourage the belief that an argument of the form "*X* is a desired end (goal, or something wanted by the agent) *Y* is a means to that end (will bring *X* about) can warrant a conclusion do *Y*" or could make doing *Y* a reasonable thing to do. But this is in some cases at least quite obviously not so, and I think never really so. Suppose that I very much want my children not to jump on their beds. We may also suppose as well that I did wish they would only take my wanting this seriously. There is no doubt, the world being what it is, that I could infallibly achieve both of those ends at one blow by breaking their legs next time they do it. But this, as anyone not corrupted by a badly assimilated course in elementary philosophy will say, is *no argument* at all for doing such a monstrous thing. The reason is, of course, obvious. It is that unless I can also argue that the state of affairs I might reach having done *Y* (or brought *Y* about) and so preventing *X* is *better* that the original state of affairs where *X* occurs without *Y* I have not given an argument for doing what I do. Generally speaking we could say that to make an account of a reasonable, good, argument for doing something in order to bring about a certain desired end even remotely plausible we would have to add to that account something to the effect that of all the ways of bringing that result about which I have envisaged *together with* the possibility that I leave well alone, what I elect to do is the best *of the alternatives*. Another way of putting this is that what is presented to me by a "means end" argument is a pattern of envisagable situations which I may be able to set before me in terms of what I know or believe about what states of affairs will have what consequences. Within that I may then make *choices*. To be sure, one may on occasion report as a means end argument a simple triad to the effect that one elected to do *Y*, or that another should so elect, just because it will bring about a desired state of affairs, but in such cases it seems all too clear this is elliptical for a larger pattern of thought. Either one has not said enough, or may be understood to have run through the other options, or perhaps cannot think of any. Often too such a report is a clear symptom of rational idleness and irresponsibility.

There is a, by no means always tacit, tendency to suppose, as Hume, for instance really seems to have done, that the role of the "will" or of preference or choice in such cases is restricted to the choice of ends, and of course it cannot be. Kant's slogan that whoever wills the ends wills the means might suggest, as it should not, that having chosen a particular end or goal one is committed to a particular choice of how to reach it: what we should say, rather, is that having chosen a particular goal we are not *thereby* exempted from the responsibility of choosing some means or other (even of rejecting all imaginable means) of reaching it. There is indeed a sense that can be given to the apparent counter-slogan, normally associated with fanatics, that the end justifies the means. Clearly, as it stands such a view is not only morally monstrous, but logically silly, but it presumably derives any persuasiveness it has from the fact that what goals we do have in mind will partially determine *how* we envisage and evaluate our more immediate actions: in particular it will determine what we take *seriously* in how we evaluate states of affairs for which we can imagine ourselves or others being responsible.

These traditional considerations aside, we can draw this general lesson from such reflections. If the topic of thought in action is partly, even from a certain point of view largely, to do with certain kinds of arguments, it is also inevitably concerned with how an agent may *attend to* and *prefer* certain things, and it is concerned with this all the way through (that is to say not merely in the restricted area of preferred *goals*). And more specifically, we can say this. A simple means-end "argument" is concerned in its application with how we may attend to what we can *imagine* or *envisage* and with how we may bring our knowledge of various sorts to bear on this.

This can set the pattern of how we may begin to consider the possibilities of exploring the limits of our standard attitudes to rationality from this point on. In this chapter I have concentrated my attention on the topic of how we are to understand the *conclusion* of a practical argument. A next step can be to turn to consider how it can be that an agent exercises his thought in practice with respect to the ways and means by which he may, he thinks or is told, be able to reach the goals, or achieve the purposes he wants and envisages. Finally, I shall turn to the question of how he understands his own goals, even to the question whether he may act intelligibly, or rationally, where is is relatively unclear what his goals are. In this way I shall adopt the triad as a method of discussion, for it can have that value however misleading it may be as a picture of a logical form. For these further topics it will be necessary to place certain questions in aesthetics at the centre of the stage.

Notes

1 Aristotle, *Ethics*, tra. J. A. K. Thomson, Penguin, 1955, p. 200.
2 Alasdair MacIntyre, *A Short History of Ethics*. Routledge, 1967 pp. 71–2.
3 Roy Edgley, *Reason in Theory and Practice*, Hutchinson, 1969, p. 28 ff where he insists that there is no way in which an *action* could be said to be the conclusion of an argument, in any sense in which "conclusion" goes along with "premise".
4 cf. *Reason in Theory and Practice*. p. 124.
This account of reason, which places the analysis of the idea of reason squarely on the back of the idea of "having reasons" is all of a piece with the position he takes on the question of an action's being the conclusion of an argument. Despite the fact that I am here arguing that it is much this line of thought that tends to underpin a certain ideological view of the place of reason in human affairs, it is important to note that Edgley is very strongly opposed to that ideological tendency himself of his paper on "Reason and Violence", *Radical Philosophy*, Spring 1973, pp. 18–24 and in a slightly shortened version in *Practical Reason* ed. Stephan Körner, Blackwell, 1974.
5 Aristotle, *Ethics* p. 200

6 J. S. Mill, *Utilitarianism*, Chapter 1.

7 cf. Alan Ryan, *The Philosophy of John Stuart Mill*, Macmillan, 1970 esp. Chapter XI.

8 For a full account of this see Ryan *op. cit.*

9 R. M. Hare, "Principles", *Proc. Aristotelian Society*, Vol. LXXIII 1972–3 p. 13. My comments may seem to be over harsh, but this paper seems to exhibit a curiously self-conscious moral philistinism which may, perhaps unfairly, be illustrated by a remark elsewhere in it (p. 9) that "Indeed it would not be too much of an exaggeration to find, in the current prevalence of fiction as an art form, the principal cause, or at least symptom, of the decline of moral standards which occasions so much concern". Perhaps if all these novels are the principal symptom of our moral decline we should not worry too much.

10 cf. Eldridge Cleaver, *Soul on Ice*, Jonathan Cape, 1969, Chap. IV. Cleaver uses this vivid expression to identify the self-congratulatory stereotype of the white American male, but it is noteworthy that it can be applied to any middle-class élitist picture of itself, e.g. that of many middle-aged middle-class dons.

CHAPTER THREE

RECIPES AND PRACTICAL PEDANTRY

It is sometimes asserted that, in principle, there could not be rules or recipes for making works of art. Indeed students studying aesthetics are sometimes asked as a stock question to consider whether such a claim might even have the status of a necessary truth. This is curious in view of the fact that such a claim is quite clearly false. It is very nearly as manifestly false as that other claim of stock aesthetics that there can be no arguments concerning matters of taste (an observation that gains nothing in plausibility from being expressed in a Latin tag *de gustibus non disputandum*). Anyone learning how to paint, write music, poetry or the skills of architecture will, whatever else he may meet, inevitably find that the learning of recipes, principles, rules of thumb and more exact rules for achieving varieties of effects and results will loom as large in his life as it would were he to undertake any less exalted trade or profession, and perhaps even more so. Perhaps someone interested in the taxonomy of rules and practical principles would do well to study the practice of education in the arts, for there he would be likely to find a greater variety of kinds of such regulative principles than anywhere else. Popular parlance tends very naturally to associate the notion of a recipe with cookery (for the reason that cooking is as close as most people get in their everyday lives to what William Morris called the "useful arts"—though he himself did not, and probably would not have included it in his own list of such things) but though cookery may well be a comparatively lowly art we would not surely for that reason deny the culinary arts any chance of being an art at all. Similarly, we may well find that on all sides people's most heated arguments can be concerned with matters of taste, whether it be with issues of "good taste" and aesthetic discernment or merely whether the cooking tastes as well as it was intended to, or the same as the cook expects and claims.

In fact, of course, these two doctrines have very similar, as well as very ancient, roots. A link between the two is often made to the extent that they can be claimed to be two aspects of the same general thesis. Somewhat parodied by compression, the thesis would be that it is the business of the "creative" artist to make what is new. His ability to rise above mere "craftsmanship" consists in doing something that goes beyond what is laid down in instruction, or can be passed on by training, and thus also to go beyond that point where established canons and standards of assessment of his success and failure can be relied on. The area of activity that he thus enters is accordingly mysterious, beyond his rational control and our rational comprehension, a world where he must rely on the Muses, his inspiration, his flair, his "mysterious" powers of expression, his gifts, where he has willingly left behind his normal rational criteria of success in projects and obedience to principles of action. If we can assess, understand, or judge him at all, once he has taken flight in this way we also must needs rely on our own flair, our inspiration and insight: when faced with art, the critic must always bear in mind that the inner light of reason gutters dimly in the winds of inspiration and that he too must place his hand in that of the Muse for guidance.

It is a way of looking at the matter that lends itself to rather purplish prose. Is this parody unfair? Well, the ingredients of this view of the arts can be found readily enough by an almost random sampling from almost any period of European thought. One does not have to concentrate on an isolated period of Romanticism. Plato asserted in the *Ion* that the artist was Muse-inspired and accordingly beyond our rational comprehension, in the un-Platonic, un-Romantic, eighteenth-century Pope was able to refer to that essential "grace beyond the reach of art" that was the mark of the true poet. By "art" he meant what today we would call "craft" and he was clearly aware of the theological overtones of "grace". That the world of artistic creativity is something set aside from mundane rationality is a *leitmotif* to a comparatively stable theme of thinking about rationality itself. It has perhaps not been noticed enough how far the very idea of what it is that an artist and critic does, or fails to do, stands as a boundary marker to a central account of thought in action and about action.

In a well known remark, Picasso once said that he wished to paint "as a bird sings". Doubtless he meant merely that he wished to paint for his own reasons, and in his own way, unfettered by externally imposed rules and regulations, unfettered by external rational constraints. He wished to paint spontaneously and for the joy of it, without ulterior motive or a view to the utilitarian purposes of his painting. But, literally understood, it is hard to imagine a more misleading analogy for what he wanted to say. The freedom of a bird is just not the sort of freedom to be original and inventive that an artist, certainly a romantic artist such as Picasso was, wished to claim. The song a robin sings is the song all robins sing. The outpourings of a lark are the same for all larks. Even those birds that imitate the songs of others do so with a slavishness, predictability and lack of invention that would make the most conservative of academic musicians fight for their independence. Song birds do not compose their songs. Neither, in any sense musicians would welcome, do they perform. For an appeal to an ideal of spontaneous freedom of artistic invention it would be hard to find a more displaced analogy. But *need all* repetition be as slavish as a bird's?

Stuart Hampshire, in an elegantly un-purple passage concerned with the difference between Moral action and evaluation and practice and judgement in the arts, has spelt out some of these connections. His starting-point is the observation that "virtue and good conduct are essentially repeatable and imitable, in a sense in which a work of art is not. To copy a right action is to act rightly; but a copy of a work of art is not necessarily a work of art." We should, he argues, beware of requiring that principles of criticism should conform to the same rational requirements as principles of conduct, "Where it makes sense to speak of a problem, it makes sense to speak of a solution to it . . . but if something is made or done gratuitously and not in response to a problem posed, there can be no question of preferring one solution to another . . . if works themselves are to be regarded as free creations, to be enjoyed or neglected for what they are, then any grading is inessential to the judgment of them."[1] His point seems to be that moral works are, in contradiction to works of art, answers to common problems which we all share, or are essentially open to those judgements and criticisms that assume that they are. Rather more oddly, it seems also to be part of his picture that creativity has no place in morality. "Where the logicians' framework of problem and conclusion does not apply, the notion of 'reason' loses some of its meaning also; it is unnatural to ask '*why* is that picture or sonata good?' in a parallel way with 'why was that a right thing to do?'. " Moral arguments, Hampshire insists, are essentially general, aesthetic ones are not, "if one generalises . . . one looks away from the particular qualities of the particular thing, and is left with some general formula or recipe, useless alike to artist and spectator. One does not need a formula or recipe unless one needs repetitions; and one needs repetitions and rules in conduct and not in art; the artist does not need a formula of reproduction and the spectator does not need a formula of evaluation." (*ibid*)

My reason for quoting this passage and discussing it in particular detail is that in many ways it can stand for just those attitudes to rationality, reasons and the arts that I have alluded to in the previous chapter while at the same time its author is one whose sympathies are not only quite un-Philistine, but who is deeply concerned with the importance of the arts as a standing challenge to what is unfeeling and bureaucratic in our society and its official moral attitudes.

Like many things that Hampshire has had to say about the arts from a philosophical point of view, this passage has the twin virtues of compression and of being highly representative of a certain commonly held point of view. Hampshire's general philosophical view of the place of both critical and artistic judgement is the very largely neo-Kantian one that aesthetic activity is in its main essentials "bracketed off" from our normal world of judgements of purposes and explanations—set apart from "science" with its concern for factual explanation and from "morality" with its concern with human welfare, and thus in this sense "gratuitous". Undoubtedly he regards the arts in this way as a "good thing", both extrinsically in that they present a constant challenge to the habits of mind engendered by the normal categories of thinking, and intrinsically too. Unlike the majority of contemporary professional philosophers, moreover, he makes good his regard for the arts by the practice of criticism in its own right. Yet it is curiously easy to imagine how these very same arguments that he uses to defend the arts from the onslaughts of those philistines who would invade the territory of the artist with irrelevant moralistic concerns might equally be used by still more aggressive philistines as grounds for despising and rejecting the fine arts altogether. For it is just the feeling that the arts are *isolated* from day to day concerns with facts and values, that in criticism the idea of "reason" loses some of its meaning, that can warrant a conviction that in a desperate world that suffers too much from the neglect of fact and human welfare, the making of a work of art is at best a mere matter of decoration and at worst a gratuitous luxury that we can ill afford, indeed that it would be irresponsible to afford. This is often enough the characteristic attitude of self consciously serious minded people, whether they be entrepreneurs, scientists or politicians. This tension is, moreover, at least as old as Plato. Shall we banish artists from the ideal republic or admire them as the possessors of some super-rational creative ability? Either way, the question presupposes that quite ordinary criteria of rationality somehow do not apply.

The feeling that this is so seems to run through a central tradition of European thought; the most respectable one withal. Even Picasso's rather odd choice of metaphor for the status of his activity in painting may be seen as a self-consciously Romantic corrollary to this tradition, for its very unclarity of thought (and it should be borne in mind that it reflects a popular cliche) can be seen as an artist's response to his sense of exclusion from normal mundane, "rational" constraints and the normal respectability that goes along with them.

Yet, if we take this passage as representative, its arguments do not seem to be very strong. This passage is concerned with repetitions. The claim is that a copy of a work of art is not similarly a work of art, in contrast to a work of virtue which may keep its virtue however often copied. This claim is, as it stands, ambiguous. There is surely no very good reason to suppose that an artefact, a made object, perhaps of great beauty, could not in principle, if not in practice, be copied many times over as a means to producing a series of equally beautiful objects. That we may find this a difficult thing to do in the case of some painting and some sculpture should not blind us to the fact that we find it easy enough to do in the case of mass produced prints, photographs, fabrics, even certain buildings; if mass production does not deal with beautiful things as often as we might like we may naturally blame designers for not doing their job well enough, not claim that their job is theoretically, let alone logically, impossible. There seems no reason in principle why mass produced objects should not be as aesthetically valuable as oft repeated actions can be morally worth while. Obscurities certainly attach to either notion, but the very idea of an aesthetically adequately produced artefact is not in principle more difficult to accept than the parallel notion in morals. Presumably however this is not what Hampshire had in mind; what he presumably had in mind was the idea that in making the thing for the second time, or the third, one would be performing a different kind of *action* from that involved in making it originally, that one would be following a recipe in this latter case but not in the former. The difference lies not in the artefact, but in the process of the agent's making it. The difference has to do with the maker's actions, not with what he makes. This can have the effect of making the task of drawing parallels with, and distinctions from, moral actions confusing. But not impossible. A moral action performed to a formula, according to a principle or recipe may be valuable for human welfare while the same action may at the same time be the expression of little or no moral virtue on the part of the agent. His thought in doing what he does may be the morally negligible one of simply doing the right thing, of slavishly copying his mentor; to distinguish between the morality of the agent in performing an action and the value of the action itself is part of the common coin of morality.

In the same way a dancer may follow the steps of a dance perfectly according to the recipe or formula laid down; that she is not inventing or designing it makes little difference to its aesthetic value as a dance. The incapacity for musical invention, creativity, even understanding, of a highly competent instrumentalist who knows how to play the notes well enough, can be notorious. Recipes, as Hampshire says, are for repetitions; to give us the works of art they do such performers have to be in the repetition business, and we may judge them as such. Is this not to judge within the context of the arts?

There are two obvious, and related replies to this. In the first place, it will be urged that mere slavish following of a formula will not result in good dancing or good playing, that it is precisely in such areas that we look for more, for an absence of pedantry, for the capacity to interpret, for a grace beyond the reach of the choreographer's instructions or of the information laid down in the musical score. Of course this is true. The question is whether this is to say something that cannot be said to some extent or another about following *any* recipe or formula. In the second place it will be urged, equally correctly, that the essential matter of making a work of art is that in *designing* it the maker cannot be following a recipe, that in inventing what is new something is involved that must go beyond, or maybe not as far as, the reach of those criteria of success and failure that have to do with rules and recipes. Again the question is whether this has anything specially to do with the arts.

So it may be as well to look a little more closely at what is in fact involved in intelligently following a recipe, and then to look more closely at what is involved in those cases where designing and inventing precedes any possibility of repetition.

A recipe is a counter-factual proposition that something or other will be the case if something else is brought about, but one which differs from other causal claims of this sort in that it is a tool in an agent's process of achieving that end. Means-end thinking is concerned inevitably with recipes. Because a recipe is a tool in that process it follows that to discover how to do something, or a new way of doing it is not to that extent to have followed a recipe. The first man to make porridge by wetting his oats, or roast pig by burning his house down followed no recipe. There is a somewhat childish puzzle about primitive skills that asks how it was that early man knew how to weave, or to make fire or pottery as if some primitive practical theorist "must" have known what to do before he started to weave. Indeed, slightly less primitive men seem traditionally to have posed some such question to themselves and supplied the answer to it that some demi-god, some Prometheus, first instructed mankind in that practical knowledge that thereafter was handed down from generation to generation. But this magical explanation of the origin of a technological theory rather clearly supplies the wrong explanation for the wrong answer to the underlying question. The assumptions behind such myths seem to be that in the case of an action and activity where the agent is not following some rule for action, some set of practical principles, some recipe, what he is doing is not rational. But, equally clearly, it is not to be despised, is not silly, not random or mad; *ergo*, his "pre-recipe" activity must be super-rational, not sub-human, but divine. The teacher who was not himself at some time a pupil must have been a demi-god.

The related ideas of invention and creativity are infected by this primitive myth. To Plato in the *Ion*, when the poet composes his work ". . . there is no invention in him until he is inspired and out of his senses, and the mind is no longer with him". Our modern English words "inspiration", even "graceful" are rooted in this ancient metaphor of the poet's being a seer in magical communication with the gods, breathing in the breath of divine wisdom or having granted to him a transcendental ability or insight into what to do. What is graceful, the grace that goes beyond the reach of what is taught or can be taught, is what cannot be captured in the repeatable, general instructions for action. It is sometimes suggested that the most obvious objection to the very idea of a poet's being Muse-inspired is that as an explanation of how he thinks in composing it is regressive, for who, after all, inspired the Muses? Other Muses, at some higher level? But this may be to miss the point both of what Plato may have had in mind and of what still lies behind the still commonplace idea that somehow or other invention, inspiration, creativity are beyond rational understanding. The point is not that we cannot give that sort of causal explanation of a person's ability to invent that merely says that he can do so because of some further fact about him (being well fed, say, or high on 'pot') but that we cannot understand what he is doing, that his rationale is beyond our comprehension, or perhaps merely, that he has no rationale, no reasons for acting in the way he does. Normally, we can offer an account of an agent's rationale—in other words understand his doing what he does—by spelling out what reasons he has for acting, what principles he is following, or what recipe he is using and to what end, but in the case of invention, or of making something new, it can be just this that we cannot appeal to in our account of his actions. As Anthony Palmer says:

> Understanding the creativity of a piece of work presents the dilemma that if the account we give is successful it will have the effect of denying that creativity is involved. The dilemma arises if it is accepted, as in general it is, that to give an account of something is to show how it might have been expected, how for example it follows from things that went before or is in accord with certain principles or standards. For this is also a plausible description of a way of denying that creativity is involved . . . How else could one deny creativity than by showing how the thing in question might have been expected or followed from certain principles? . . . If the same is pointed to in denying creativity as is pointed to in giving an account of it, it is not surprising that it tends to disappear with its own account. The element of originality might still be left, of being the first to work in terms of certain principles, but then, to understand the creativity involved would be to understand how those principles came to be used and the dilemma returns.[2]

Perhaps "dilemma" is a misnomer here. There certainly can seem to be a fairly stark option here, but the very idea that inspiration, grace, gracefulness, inventiveness, are frequently seen to be beyond our rational understanding shows that for many one of the options can be accepted happily enough. Indeed, why should it not be a mark of good sense, and of good philosophical sense, moreover, to see that reason, and thus rationality and the possibility of rational understanding of an agent's actions, has bounds? If a "lower" boundary is that marked by silliness, fooling about, random scatty activity, at the other end of the scale there is that that goes "beyond" "mere" principle-following, where there are rules for action for achieving certain ends into an area that it is free of such constraints. It surely is a form of proper respect for rationality to show a proper respect for the limited scope of reason. If we adopt that view of reason in action that makes a rational action just that which accords with some rule both accepted by the agent as the rule of his action and derivable from more general principles,[3] we will have to conclude that what does not accord with such principles of action must be essentially opaque to our understanding—a conclusion that many are very willing to accept, and to accept as a compliment to artistry in practice.

There are several different issues here. The first time a maker of something invents or designs it, clearly he cannot, so long as by "recipe" we mean a set of instructions for repeating something, be following a recipe. It can be a quite separate question whether he is or is not following any practical principles at all, and a different question again whether he is being silly but fortunate, benefiting from that sort of casual serendipity granted to the inventor of roast pig, or shows great intelligence, thought and concentration. To discover by chance that something or other that one had done has produced a delightful effect, and then to set out to repeat the process is a different thing entirely from setting out to design something or to invent a way of achieving something. To set out to discover a way of achieving something that one very clearly has in mind as a goal is a different thing again from designing or composing something where it is an essential part of the business that before one has completed the design one is not yet certain what result will be the successful conclusion. On the whole we tend to refer most often to "creativity" in these latter sorts of situations and to "invention" in the former. The fact that this is at best only roughly the case may indicate either that our normal idioms do not reflect any great clarity on the part of standard users of such idioms about just where these distinctions really cut, or it may indicate that the differences can on occasion be pretty marginal. But surely in neither case are there externally laid down practical principles for achieving such things, and surely there are not recipes for inventing or designing. However, if we are to accept the challenge of understanding these sorts of activities we will need to know much more than that and to investigate these distinctions much more closely.

A rough way of distinguishing the two sorts of inventiveness can be to say that "invention" has to do with those cases where the agent "knows" his goal but not his means, while "creativity" refers to a more puzzling sort of case (but I shall go on to argue, still a familiar one) where the problems have to do with the fact that in some central sense the agent is not fully aware of his own goal. Just as there is a philosophical issue concerned with the very idea of an agent's conclusion to a practical argument, there are corresponding problems concerned with the agent's grasp of its premises. A feeling that neither invention nor creativity can be understood in rational terms can be the result simply of a feeling that these problems are sufficiently intractible to forbid the very idea of a practical principle and thus the very idea of thought in action, being applied in such cases. But we need more than a feeling to go on. Let us take "invention" first.

Even where the agent does know what he wants, and does have before him instructions about how to reach that goal, instructions which he accepts and is determined to follow, there may still be a question, which is very like a question of rationality, about his practical good sense in how he follows the recipe. For it is possible to follow a recipe well or badly, with block-headed pedantry or with ease and grace. Just as there is more to playing music than playing the notes, so there is more to following any instruction for achieving a repeatable effect than reading it, marking it, even learning it and putting it into practice.

It is sometimes supposed that the fact that to follow a dance, a choreographer's instructions, or to play a piece of printed music requires that one should contribute something oneself, some "grace" that goes beyond the reach of what is laid down, shows something about these cases having to do with the arts, albeit the interpretive arts, that the "artistry" of the performer has to do with what cannot be caught in the instruction-to-repeat and that in this respect these cases are special. But there can be a muddle here. Certainly it is the case that a great deal of printed music for example, should properly be regarded as setting a framework for the musician's performance rather than complete instructions for it. There may be places in the score, such as breaks for cadenzas, where it is an essential part of what the player is told to do that he is told to make up something not laid down, to invent at that point. Not all scores may be as "open" as that, but even where the composer has written down as much as he can as fully as he can the player will still have to know how to interpret what he reads, will have to know and to be skilled in the right style of playing for the particular piece, and he will have to have some view on that matter even if (perhaps particularly if) such issues are a matter for dispute among different players. The difference between a good and a very bad performance of a piece may embrace a variety of cases where all the notes that are printed, and all the instructions for playing them that are printed, are followed. Hence the difference between a good and a very bad performance cannot be spelt out in the score and, it might be concluded, hence such a score is not a recipe for the repetition of a certain result since the playing of music is an art form, the creativity the flair of the player, his artistry are in a special case. Such a conclusion would be mistaken.

Certainly, it would be absurd to argue that a player of a score is not engaged in something special in the way of what is demanded of him in terms of interpretive imagination and skill, but it would be equally wrong to conclude from this that to a similar, if a more humble, extent very much the same does not apply to what it is to follow any recipe. No recipe can itself contain instructions for how it should be followed. Some element of invention must be involved in following any recipe.

A recipe for making something is an intellectual tool in the process of making, and as such can be used well or badly. As written, a recipe is a piece of theory, the theoretical claim that by doing such and such a certain result will follow. In this sense a printed score of music can be regarded as a theoretical claim that these notes in these orders will amount to the work concerned. But following any recipe is a practical matter and the understanding involved in following it is essentially practical understanding. Just as with the appalling, but "correct" player, it is possible to follow any recipe, but to follow it so pedantically, so unimaginatively and stupidly, that the agent's actions, though all in some sort of sense rather literally in accordance with the rules for conduct are quite silly enough to be in any common sense of the word "irrational". But the recipe itself will not be able to state the criteria of rationality, irrationality, silliness or sense involved.

If recipes are practical they are for the practical use of the materials with which they are concerned. To be able to understand that is to be able to understand the materials. Not to do so is to follow the recipe (in a thin and "literal" sense) but to follow it without understanding. The pattern of a recipe as a means-end argument can suggest that all that is involved in following a recipe is for the agent to know what he wants to achieve, know from the recipe what has to be done to achieve it, and thus doing that. In this spirit the picture of the matter could be given by the sample "Make a batter pudding. Batter puddings are made by putting these and these ingredients into a bowl, doing this and that with them, etc., so do all that." But even if the recipe is very explicit indeed there will still be different ways in which "all that" can be done. A newly wed housewife read in her new recipe book that in order to make a certain sort of flaky pastry it is necessary to roll out a paste to the thickness of an eighth of an inch, lay onto the rolled out paste inch cubes of butter at two inch intervals, fold and roll, and repeat the process. Using the ruler and set square borrowed from her husband's new carpentry set, she attempted with the greatest possible care to follow what the book told her to do, and was most disappointed with the results of her efforts.[4] It may be objected that no philosopher who has been concerned with arguments of means to ends could have supposed that the bare schema of a typical means-end argument should be interpreted so pedantically, that of course, just as it is necessary to follow a recipe for making flaky pastry with unpedantic good sense, so the schematic samples of arguments offered by philosophers need to be understood equally unpedantically. But this can be a dangerous way of philosophising. Without due care whole truths may fall through the gaps between a bare schematic theory and the practice of real life. The important truth that can be lost sight of here is that the theoretical instruction of how to achieve something needs to be followed in so far as it is compatible with the natural way in which the materials behave: it is about materials. A manual of flower arranging may suggest that a certain effect can be achieved by placing the flowers in an equilateral triangle; it is just *not* to follow the manual to see this as requiring that they be placed with the precision of a frame of snooker balls. Not only will flowers not go that way, but even if, with some effort they were forced to, the effect would not be what the manual intends. The most carefully written handbook or recipe book cannot preempt the experience of and sensitivity to materials that is required for putting it into practice. Pastry is not plywood any more than flowers are billiard balls. To have a sense of what materials a given recipe may have to do is a *precondition* for using a recipe; it cannot be a part of a recipe, or of any other practical principle to spell that out. Equally, there has to be a limit to the extent to which further practical advice can take the place of what can only be known in the experience of using materials. It is sometimes said that to make well is to have a "feeling" for materials, but we should not be misled by the emotional overtones of "feeling" in such an idiom.

It is a commonplace of talk about the practical activities of artists in making what they do to refer to their "feeling" for their materials, to a sculptor's feeling for clay or stone or wood, to a poet's feeling for words. And it seems to be quite generally agreed that in some way that is quite central to our understanding and judgement of the arts, to lack such a "feeling" is a sufficient guarantee of failure in these callings. But the idea of "feeling" here is not always very clear. Of course it is and should be central to that idea that an emotion of sorts is involved, and often a very powerful one. It is indeed part of a sculptor's feeling for his materials that he should like the feel of what he handles, even have an affection for the stuff of his craft that can, often without exaggeration, be *like* being in love with wood or stone or steel. Of course this is an emotional matter, sometimes deeply and violently so, but we make a great mistake if we conclude from this that it is only or merely that. For this is perhaps above all an area of human experience where it is *fundamentally* a mistake to suppose that a category of emotion excludes a category of thought. A "feeling for materials" is a feeling right enough, but it is a feeling that directs *attention* and concentrates choice and judgement in a particular and often highly specific manner, and these are intellectual matters. As we have seen, a schema of that sort of practical thinking is conveniently construed as a means-end argument may also be seen as a schema of choice and attention to what has to be chosen, or can be envisaged as chosen. Attention to materials where a recipe is being followed (where a means-end "argument" is being put to use) is thus *at the same time* attention to the interpretation of the recipe—to what it *means* in practice. This is a fact that is in no way confined to practice in the arts, to "aesthetic" matters, even though it can be easiest to investigate it in that context. It is perhaps above all of importance in moral contexts where practical *thought* has to do with a feeling for people, the "materials" of moral thought in action.

To make a mistake about the material conditions of a practical principle's application is to make an *intellectual* mistake, a mistake in understanding, for that such a principle cannot itself take the place of a concern for, and a close attention to, the materials with which it is concerned is a logical fact. It is closely related to the situation with borderline cases and exceptions to such practical principles as laws and regulations. Suppose a university department requires that a certain piece of work should be submitted at a certain time, but also does not wish to automatically penalise all those who may in one way or another nonculpably fail to meet the deadline. It would, of course, be perfectly possible for the rule to be enforced so strictly that any work handed in for whatever reason even a few minutes after the deadline will be considered "void", but in this case there is a genuine desire to temper the wind to the shorn lamb. Now, though it is possible to have some general principles about what sort of excuses will not be accepted, it is just not possible *in principle* to lay down absolutely complete necessary and sufficient conditions for what constitutes a relevantly shorn lamb. If a broken leg or a bad case of the 'flu counts as a good excuse for lateness, what about a quite bad cold, or a week of moderate depression over a domestic upset? These things can quite reasonably interfere with someone's work, but they can also, notoriously be given as poor excuses by idle students. One might well imagine in such a case (indeed one may actually find) some student feeling most aggrieved that the authorities do not come clean and spell out in advance which of those excuses will count and what will not, but if it really is the intention of the administrators to take care that people are not treated arbitrarily such a requirement can only lead to the possibility of new borderline cases for which there may have to be further regulations. The regress is both logically and, if seriously pursued, morally vicious. In the case of more simply descriptive borderlines the situation is plainer still. Someone required to sort objects into sets of different, but adjacent, colours cannot in principle expect that the instructions can cover any object that is a colour just between the two, and any further refinement of the instruction can only result in a new borderline. But the matter has not only to do with this familiar feature of descriptive borderlines.

In each case the description incorporated in the practical rule or principle requires that at some point in its application the agent has to make a judgement there and then what to do that is not itself directed by the principle, though *that* he has to is so directed. For this reason it cannot be an objection to a practical principle that it does not fully legislate for whether it applies or fails to apply in any given case. Though it might be possible to interpret an examination regulation so "tightly" that there is in *practice* no problem about deciding borderlines, this is even then at best a practical likelihood (there, after all, could be agonies over micro-second delays, and even the toughest minded legislator would regard some such agonies as silly). No prior legislation will avoid the possibility of intermediate cases. The important further point is that to understand the principle at all it is necessary also to have some conception of what sorts of borderline or indeterminate cases it can permit. Often this is a matter of how "rough" or otherwise the descriptions in the principle should be taken to be. But it is misleading to see this as if it were a matter of paying attention to the *principle*. It is a matter of paying attention to the world it must be applied in. In general the more attention to the circumstances of a principle's application it invites, or requires, the less the principle alone can preempt the necessity of attention and judgement in its application. There is a familiar sense of "practical" in which a principle may be said to be more practical as it requires more attention to the material world rather than to language in its use. In this sense the more practical a principle may be the greater will be the danger, and absurdity of, pedantry in its use.

I once asked a builder of Cotswold dry stone walls to teach me how the job was done. The "theory" of a dry stone wall's construction is both interesting in that it relies on some quite general principles, and, with some reflection, relatively easy to state. Generally, it is a matter of placing longer and heavier stones on smaller and lighter ones in such a way that the former hold down and tie in the latter both along the length of the wall and across it, while the smaller stones provide packing and stability. There are some traditional terms of art that describe that process in more refined detail, but not very many. But walling stone is undressed and is used in relatively random plates of varying thickness. No stone has a very obviously straight side. The well built wall, however, seems to be quite miraculously smooth sided and even. It seemed a natural, inevitable, question for the somewhat wide eyed amateur to ask how this was achieved, how the builder knew what stone to put where, and in particular what edge of the stone to place on the outside. The answer was simple enough; there are two things to remember, never, after picking the stone up put it down except onto the wall, and that the stone decides the right way for it to go. To any philosopher, in Austin's phrase, "cap and categories in hand", to say that the stone decides can seem quite obviously at worst picturesque and absurd or at best an elliptical way of saying that the builder decides what to do with the stone with the stone in his hand, as he handles it. But this is at best only a partial interpretation. Clearly, nobody need suppose than an inanimate object such as a stone in fact engages in mental processes of any sort, still less comes to decisions, and in that sense it is obvious that it is the maker that decides, not the materials he is using, and it is only slightly less obvious that he can only decide what to do with the stone with the background knowledge of how walls are built that corresponds to what he can be told, but that information may still mean very little "in the abstract", apart from the actual business of making the thing itself. The notions of relative weights and sizes of stones need to be understood in terms of their feel in the hand, how they can hold each other together in terms of the sensation of their dragging each other as they are placed, and so on. The background knowledge that can be expressed in a handbook on methods of wall building is in a large part a direction of a way of paying attention to the stones and the feeling of handling them, and conversely to understand what the handbook means (the relevant senses of "heavy" and "large", for example) is to apply the general instructions to actual or recalled experience of paying attention to the objects involved. To be absorbed in a practical activity of this sort that is going well is for there to be no real distinction between the judgement that a certain stone will do well at a certain place and the experience of so placing it and its not feeling out of place. To make such a judgement without the stone in one's hand is to have to imagine what it might feel like to be so placed; that is a possible, useful, sometimes essential thing to do, but one may imagine wrong. The verification of what it is that one has in fact decided, as well as that the decision was a good one in terms of the larger project, must ultimately depend on the matter of handling the stuff itself.

To some degree or another this is generally true of any practical principle, any theory of what has to be done, and in this way what the rules for action in fact amount to can only be understood in terms of what must necessarily be *particular* experience. It is, of course, trivially true that to succeed in building a wall or making an omelette, or arranging a vase of flowers, is to succeed in making a particular wall, and so on, but the point goes further than this. It is that the final check on what the principles of action themselves amount to, what they mean, the degree of "roughness" or precision of the terms involved is similarly particular.

This fact is in no way confined to those practical principles that have to do with the arts, nor indeed to those that have to do with "craftsmanship". It equally applies to the practical principles of morals. Moral principles, perhaps pre-eminently, require to be understood in terms of the material conditions of their application. The moral pedant who, believing that it is always wrong to tell lies doggedly insists on telling the exact truth when asked his his opinion of his wife's new coat or his children's schoolwork is not following his principles scrupulously, but idiotically, and to that extent is failing to follow them, not succeeding. A common way of dealing with this sort of case from the philosophical point of view is to say that what this unpleasant person should have done was to adopt a different principle in the first place, say the rule not to say what is false unless it is tactless to do so, or not to tell lies except to deceive the enemy and so on.[5] But this won't do. Qualified by exclusion clauses or not, a principle needs to be applied in action in particular circumstances. Truth telling is at least as subtle a matter as laying stones to build a wall, because any communication is; to know what it is that I am asked truly to tell when I am asked for my opinion on a child's painting or arithmetic is to know something about children and that child, something about painting or arithmetic and that painting or arithmetic as well as to know what 'in the abstract' I think about it. It is unrealistic to sharply divide these sorts of knowledge from each other. No amount of qualifying clauses for the general principle can preempt my taking notice of these things: a general principle is general in that it may be applied to many particular cases, but the cases themselves are no less particular. It is an error to suppose that because any general principle has to be applied to particular cases it is thereby *not* a general principle (any more than the principles of wall building are) and it is very much the same error in reverse to suppose that the requirements of attention to the actual conditions of a principle's practice can be taken care of by further and further modifications of the principle itself. The former error is that which tends to dog the footsteps of those who are concerned with the arts where it tends to be held that *because* success in performance must be particular there cannot be general principles of action. The latter is the error of pedantic formalism in morals. They are natural bedfellows.

It is easy enough to find people who, while holding the most enlightened moral principles, strong-willed and vigorous, rarely given to thinking that they really ought to do something and not able to get around to doing it, are at the same time moral incompetents. They suffer from the moral equivalent of kack-handedness. They are either unable or are unwilling to pay attention to the material, particular circumstances of their principles' application. A wood worker who does not like the feel of wood, or who is shy of it, will be unable to pay attention to what he is doing, will never get the practical knowledge he has been instructed in into the "living texture" of what he does. In morality one needs a "feeling for materials" too. Though I have the moral principles of angels and have no affection for the circumstances of their application, my works will be vain.

I have in the foregoing paragraphs used the expressions "recipe" "practical principle" and "rule" without distinguishing between them, and this is because the point about the particular conditions of their practical application does not require such a distinction, but the notions of generality and openness of a rule or principle do require some distinctions, particularly if they are to be applied in the practical contexts of making things.

The word "rule" is perhaps one of the most slippery in the whole of standard philosophical vocabulary: it suggests a clarity of sense that it does not have. Perhaps the most nearly adequate statement of what a rule is is that it is a proposition to the effect that something or other is correct or incorrect, and the best that can be said for such a "definition" is that it is, at all events, adequately vague. It is vague on three central counts: what is meant by "proposition" here, what it is to follow, or to be guided by a rule in this sense, and the twin, or at least opposed, questions of correctness and incorrectness. Perhaps the most that one can say is that to be acquainted with the rules for something or other is to know what would be correct or incorrect, and this can cover a multitude of different cases. To be aware of any regulative principle at all, however precise or imprecise, general or specific is in this not quite vanishingly weak sense, to have a rule for action. This may explain the popularity of talk about rules, but it does so by indicating how many questions may be begged by such talk.

Of the three questions raised by this notion the most commonly discussed are the first two, those of explicitness and guidance. It is, for instance, often supposed that to use a language is to engage in a "rule governed activity", which *can* mean very little more than that it is possible to use the right words sometimes and the wrong words at other times. But the very idea that language could be rule-governed is sometimes objected to on the grounds that it leads to a regress. The regress is that if the claim that language is rule-governed is to mean anything it must mean that the sense of any particular expression must depend on their being some set of linguistic rules; but then, it is argued those rules must make sense, and so on *ad infinitum*. What such an objection assumes is that to be in possession of a rule is either to have stated, or to be able to state something or other of the appropriate sort as a condition of following the rule.

This assumption can have a strong and a weak force. In the strongest sense the assumption would be that a rule must be *a statement* to the effect that something or other was correct or that something or other was incorrect, much as a boarding-house landlady might pin up a set of rules for the conduct of the guests numbered one to ten, or as a boxed game might print the rules on the inside of the box. A weaker assumption would be that the agent of such an activity could, whenever challenged say what rule was being followed or what contravened and thus infer from such a statement that a certain course of action was "against the rules". Clearly, neither of these things will do for the idea of language, or for many similar sorts of activities, being rule-governed. The first assumption clearly leads to a formal regress, while the second is false. Most speakers can readily enough recognise when any word or expression is used incorrectly, but are quite unable to state a rule of language from which its incorrectness follows. (If it were a condition of rationality that the agent must be able to formulate some rule or principle from which his conclusion that a particular action was correct or incorrect, we would have to conclude that the activity of either incorrectly or correctly speaking a language was irrational.) As we have seen, very much the same thing can apply to any skill or procedure, however orderly it may be; the maker of walls, a carpenter, any craftsman, may have to reflect at length and with difficulty before he can formulate the principles on which he operates. In each case "knowing" that what one did was right or wrong can quite standardly precede being able to formulate any rule. Alternatively the formulations of the various rules and procedures may have been long forgotten while the knowledge of what to do when may not have at all, indeed the latter may, characteristically often will, be what is responsible for forgetting the former. A fluent speaker of a foreign language may have forgotten the rules that he originally learnt as consequence of his fluency.

For these reasons it might be supposed that the very idea of a rule, or practical principle is misplaced in this context since, even on the weakest assumption of such a principle being formulable, the knowledge of what is correct or otherwise will turn out to be what produces the rules, and not contrariwise. To be sure, the notion of rules and principles will still have a place, but that place will be concerned with the business of grammarians, of teachers, or of those legislators who may analyse and justify what people may already do, not with talkers, makers and everyday practical agents. The question remains however whether there is any residual concept of rule or principle that can still have a value for practice itself.

One question we may ask about rules and rule-following, (which seems to have been Wittgenstein's) can be what it can mean to say that an agent, in particular someone engaged in the activity of calculating or inferring, can be "forced" or guided by the rules even though he may be unable to formulate them;[6] clearly this can be a fairly direct way into the traditional problem of philosophy that is concerned with the status of the principles of logic and mathematics in our thinking, but in the case of most practical principles, whether they be those of morals or those for making things, we would not say in any case that the agent was forced or compelled to follow them. A related question that is less often discussed does enter these areas however. That is the question of what it is to "know" or to recognise that something is correct or is incorrect in what one is doing.

Certain sorts of practical principles or rules are such that to follow them is to know at any time that some action or state of affairs is correct and that some other alternative would be incorrect, and *vice versa*. If, for example, there is a rule of a game to write the letters A, C, K, L at a certain point, then doing that is correct, while to do anything else, e.g. to write Q, R,V,Y is incorrect. Copy typing might be construed in this manner. The instructions are that the typist should do something quite specific which will be correct, and accordingly, for her to type anything else will be incorrect. We can say that in such a case knowledge of what is right is exactly "flanked" by knowledge of what would be wrong. It is a characteristic of such cases that we can report a failure to follow the practical principles as an *error*, and as Austin pointed out, the etymology of the word can be illuminating, since to err is to stray, to stray, that is, from some predetermined line. An even clearer case of the possibility of this sort of error would accordingly be tracing a line, and it is a logical feature of such cases that to claim that something or other is wrong is to be in a position to claim what would not have been.

But such cases are comparatively rare. I may know well enough that a word I have used is not the right one to express what I mean while being in no position to say what would have been the right one. On another occasion I may know perfectly well that something I have done was right without having any very clear idea at all about what other sorts of things I could have done would not have been. To know that what I said, how I have arranged the decoration in my room, how I have placed the last stone on a wall, or the final touch of flavouring in a stew may be to know perfectly well that what I have done was all right while having at best only the most general knowledge of what would not have been. Clearly I will be able to say that some things would not have done at all, would have been clearly silly, but I may know no more in that way than if I still had failed to get the thing right.

It seems natural to suppose that where such knowledge is "flanked" will be confined to cases which, like tracing or copying, involve precise prior instructions of what to do, cases which are not like most recipes but which are like the instructions for painting by numbers. It is a characteristic of such cases that they are not only concerned with repetition but that they are concerned with specific repetition, are not concerned with *general* principles for doing things, whether they be principles of morality or of cookery. Useful recipes, on the other hand, are for certain sorts, kinds, types of things; a recipe for a certain dish is for a certain type of dish, not for an exact duplicate of a particular meal. It is an important logical fact that the business of following principles, recipes or practical rules for achieving some end or making some artefact involves the exercise of thought and judgement of a sort that cannot be preempted by the practical principles themselves. Neither the rules of language nor the practical principles or specific recipes of cookery are instructions for rote performance or ritual recitation.

Rote performance or recitation is in a central sense "mindless" in just that sense in which ordinary speaking, performing, or recipe following (whatever the wide differences between these activities may be) is not. The mindlessness is that which has to do with the idea of an action or activity being *stereotyped*. There is, however, no doubt that stereotyped linguistic or other performances can be justified by being in accord with rules or principles for what should be done; from a certain point of view it can even seem paradigmatic of such principle or rules following that the agent can justify what he did by appealing to the principle or rule that just what he did should have been done on just that sort of occasion. Any account of an agent's rationality that relies *simply* on his having or being able to give reasons for what he does when he acts, which does not distinguish between such stereotyped behaviour and other sorts of behaviour that may be justified by reference to practical principles is likely to give the very idea of an agent following practical principles a not wholly unjustified bad name. Without taking account of any difference between stereotyped rule-governed behaviour and less mindless activities it is hard to see, for example, how we might distinguish between that monster of a certain kind of moral depravity, the man who having a certain moral code, simply puts it into practice, or that monster of practical idiocy who attempts to do "just what the handbook says" and any intelligent sensitive practical agent doing his best with the knowledge he has, beyond saying that such monsters know better, because more exactly, what to do. To speak by rote on the appropriate occasions is certainly to know just what to say, but such a state of practical knowledge should hardly be the goal of one who would use his own language with precision. Though it might be to speak as a bird sings. The very idea of such a goal for linguistic, or any other sort of practical competence, would rest on an absurdity, the absurdity of supposing that any practical rule or principle that is general and flexible enough to be useful to guide action, could preempt thought in its application. It is simply a mistake to suppose that because no rule for the usage of normal language in normal situations, however well-formulated, could save the speaker the trouble of thinking what he should say, or however well understood, insure him against not knowing on some occasions what he should say. Principles for action of this sort do not work like that.

The above paragraph is deliberately general. Can we say more clearly what general principles for action of this sort have in common that distinguishes them from rules for stereotyped repetition? I think that we can and that the best way of doing so is to return to the notion of repetition in the arts, for we may find a useful model of the issue involved in the idea of the difference between a slavish, and a non-slavish performance of say, a piece of music or a play. Why, we might ask, are excellent and accurate performances still not rote, and mindless, repetitions, for it is surely intuitively obvious that they are not?

It is trivial enough that insofar as language may communicate thought, is the central device whereby people express what they mean to others, nothing could be a language in any sense worthy of the name that was so well regulated that it preempted a speaker's thinking what to say *in* his saying. (Such well-regulated, degenerate "languages" do exist of course, for instance in certain sorts of ritualised situations. There a speaker may think *about* what he should say, whether he should perform the ritual, whether he has the words right, but it may not matter for all that even whether he can understand the words, since it is not a matter of *his* meaning them, but only of his meaning to perform the ritual.)

It may be objected, however, that in saying these rather general things I am driving the connections between speaking and other sorts of activities too hard, that in particular too much should not be made of a connection between moral and linguistic thought and thought in the arts. For one way of regarding the *products* of the arts is to see them as objects in their own right with a life of their own such that, in direct contrast with the normal "productions" of a speaker they do not need to be understood in terms of their being the expression of thought of whoever produced them. (Much the same objection has often been made to a view, which while resembling the one I am pressing for, is not mine, namely that such works are the expression of their makers' feelings or emotions.) Can we not, for instance, regard a piece of sculpture, a picture, even a poem, as having the value it does *independently* of who produced it, his thought in doing so, his intentions, and so on? It has often been urged that to speak of the artist's intentions or thought in making what he did is a folly of critical judgement (commits an "intentionalist fallacy") that draws our interest unwarrantably away from what should be the true subject of our concerns in responding to the arts—the *work* itself—towards a search for a psychological will-o'-the-wisp. I have already argued that so long as we can regard any product as successful—as being what the agent meant to say or do—this is an anxiety that need not concern us, however, it is in one way true—though trivially so—that we might suppose any object, sculpture, poem, even a letter, as having come about by chance, by natural processes without the agency of any maker. What is not trivial, but I think not true either, is that in regarding something as a work of art ought properly to be regarded we can at the same time suppose this. Of course it is open to anyone to coin the expression "regarding something aesthetically" to mean regarding it as if it were irrelevant how it came to be. Then he would have to show that the proper way of regarding a work of art was "aesthetically" and that would be another matter altogether.

For even though there may be difficulties involved in the idea of a maker's thought in producing what he does (which are in many ways the topic of this book) my concern with those difficulties at least partly derives from a conviction that works of art and similar artefacts are, despite obvious differences, objects of *communication* and that the peculiar problems of understanding that they can present derive from the fact that we need to understand them thus. If, for instance, we are to understand Picasso's works, made in his terms "as a bird sings", we will certainly not have to look for a "message" or an ulterior purpose in what he was doing, but we will have to look at what his making "as a bird sings" really amounts to. A way of putting this is to ask what he was doing, what as one idiom has it, his "design" was.

In many ways that idiom can be seen as central, for the two ideas of what a maker's design may be and of what the design of what he made was are, while clearly different, closely linked. They are linked at the point of the idea of how we recognise and identify an object as a designed artefact, and it is to that we should turn next if we are to go further along the road towards an understanding of the nature of a maker's thought.

Notes

1 cf. Stuart Hampshire, "Logic and Appreciation" reprinted in Elton, *Aesthetics and Language* Blackwell, 1959, pp. 161–9.
2 cf. "Creativity and Understanding", Aristotelian Society, Sup. Vol., July 1971. The issues in this paper and in my reply to Palmer in the same volume provide the starting-point for much contained here and in subsequent chapters.
3 cf. Ryan, *loc. cit.*
4 This refers to an actual case: the result was not unlike a kind of brittle ravioli.
5 cf. Hare, "We do not say 'speak the truth in general, but it doesn't matter if what you say is false once in a way'; we say rather 'speak the truth in general but there are certain *classes* of cases where this principle does not hold' ", *Language of Morals,* p. 51. Even if we do say all this it won't guard against moral pedantry: on the contrary to suppose that it can do so will tend to encourage just such pedantry.
6 cf. *Philosophical Investigations,* Blackwell, 1953; and *Remarks on the Foundations of Mathematics,* Blackwell, 1956.

CHAPTER FOUR

DESIGNED OBJECTS

THE idea that works of art can be considered as type objects has, in the words of a recent commentator[1] acquired something of a consensus among many of us who have written on Aesthetics in the last two decades, and I shall not, accordingly, repeat the discussion at any length. However, some rather sketchy outline of the issues involved is necessary in this context since it is with some of the corollaries of this view that I wish to be concerned here. The technical distinction between the idea of a type object and something's being a particular token, or instance, of that type can be marked most shortly by recalling Pierce's account of how we identify, how we may count, words. Briefly, the point can be illustrated by remarking that the question how many words the English sentence "Our cat bit their cat" contains, is ambiguous. The question could equally well be answered by saying that the sentence contains five words or by saying that it contains four words. If we say that the sentence contains four words what we will have in mind is that the *single* word "cat" occurs in the sentence twice: the two instances of that word's occurrence are the two distinguishable "piles of ink" that in this case occur second and fifth in this row of "piles of ink". It is important that we can count words differently in this way. To claim that a book is so many thousand words long is, for instance, a claim about word *tokens* whereas to claim that a certain language, say Basic English, has so many thousand words in it is a claim about word *types:* it would be a mean sort of a philosophical error that required that a compositor who set the type of the Bible in Basic English should not be paid for more than five thousand words type setting on the grounds that that language does not contain more than that number of words—typesetters set tokens, not types.

Clearly, this rather trivial example is to scratch the surface of a very general and rather complex issue, but one thing that seems to stand out from even such a simplistic example as this is that these different ways of counting such things as words has to do with what it is to count as a thing of a certain kind, and in particular may have to do with criteria of identity for certain sorts of things that seem to depart from normal criteria of material object identity. To put the matter briefly, the very same word may very easily, so long as it is the word-type that we have in mind, be seen, or be located at many different places at the same time, something that no material object can be. Quite clearly, just the same may be said of those sorts of things, such as books or poems, that are "made of" words: I may very well have the very same book on my shelf as you have on yours, notwithstanding that we each possess different material objects. But, equally clearly, what does for books and poems may do for all sorts of other things. I may have the very same gramophone record as you, the same photograph, car, dinner service, even live in the same house, without in any of these cases sharing the same material objects. The Span House, or the Rolls-Royce Silver Ghost, the Concorde and so on are proper names whose references are not to particular material objects, but to the type objects of which certain buildings, cars and individual aeroplanes are the instances or tokens. That I may see the very same play, or hear the very same symphony as you at the same time but in different places would, accordingly, seem to be a simple species of this quite general phenomenon.

An advantage of recognising this is that certain apparently puzzling features of our talk about the arts can at least be seen as not unusual or peculiar to the arts. Not seeing this can invite a state of mind about the arts that sees the very idea of a work of art as unduly mysterious. What can seem to be mysterious is the fact that while it is perfectly obvious that it is a necessary condition of being acquainted with (say) a piece of music that I should be able to hear, or of a play or a painting that I should (among other things) be able to see, our ways of identifying and counting such things do not seem to accord with standard and familiar ways of identifying and counting audible or visible items of the world's furniture. This can generate the somewhat specious dilemma that inclines us to say both that works of art are somehow "imaginary" objects, which pays a compliment to the fact that it is not always a condition of locating or counting them that they should be located or counted in the ways that material objects are, while at the same time they are in some rather obvious ways objects of sense experience. This dilemma can at least seem to be more obviously spurious by noting that just the same thing can be said about all sorts of other things that are given proper names in our culture, such as pound notes, Union Jacks and, of course, words.

As this stands, however, it might well be objected that to generalise a problem is not to solve it, that all such an association of issues can show is that the problem may be a greater one than we might have supposed. It might also be objected that by the same token to associate central topics about works of art with a general issue about what might be called cultural objects is to have a recipe for losing sight of whatever may be special about works of art.[2] What is needed is some exploration of what is really involved in this sort of distinction.

Central to what is involved in the idea of works of art being type objects is what might be called "essential reproducibility". A piece of music, or a play, or a poem is "essentially reproducible" in the somewhat punning sense that it is essential to its being the sort of thing that it is that it should be reproducible at all events in principle, while it is at the same time part of what is meant by reproducibility in this sense that the object is reproducible in essentials. It is perhaps not frequently enough noticed that one may still sing the very same tune as another person, still have the very same poem on one's bookshelf as him, or for that matter have the very same dinner set or car, despite the fact that in singing the tune one may sing it differently, even with a few wrong notes, that the two printings of the poem may vary in identifiable ways, and the individual cars or pieces of crockery may also vary quite markedly. To put the matter somewhat over simply, we show what we take that poem or that tune, etc. to be to a large extent by what we take to be unimportant variations of this sort. Rather generally, the concept of a type object has built into it criteria of what the important, central, features, any token instance should be that can permit it to be an instance of the type in question; the equivalent claim that two objects are each cases of the same type (in this general way we often in such cases say simply "the same thing") is not simply that they resemble each other to some high degree, but that they resemble each other in relevant ways, and our understanding of what the type in question is can be spelt out in terms of our criteria of relevancy.

For example, all sorts of different inscriptions may be accepted as instances of the same word. There may be enormous variations in how we can make marks on the surfaces of things in such a way that our doing so can constitute our writing the word "cat". There is moreover, all the difference in the world between someone writing the word "cat" badly and his failure to write the word at all. To learn to write a word well, or to speak it well, is largely a matter of learning to copy certain standard, normal ways of writing the word—standard tokens of the word—with reasonable accuracy, but the type word is not such a standard instance, since the type itself is not a token. The word "cat" identified in the manner that has it that the sentence "Our cat bit their cat" can indeed be written, but it cannot be copied: that sort of resemblance holds between tokens or instances. To suppose otherwise, to identify types, say with paradigm instances—as it might be the best written inscription of the word in question—can fairly easily be seen to generate something of a vicious regress. For if what all writings of the word "cat" have in common is that they are all writings of the same word, what are we to say of the paradigm instance? Either it is an instance of it is not. If it is not, then it is hard to see how it could at the same time be a best instance. If it is, then what is it an instance of? The only answer would seem to be that it instantiates itself, but this can be puzzling too, for most instances of types are material objects of the sort that can be changed and damaged (as in this case we can erase a word), and if such an object is a best instance then less good instances will resemble it in those various ways in which material objects can resemble one another, so it also might be changed or damaged. Then we would either have to say that all the other inscriptions of the word in question ceased to be inscriptions of that word, or that there was some further paradigm that our first case was itself an instance of and which all the others instantiate. Clearly we can repeat this set of moves indefinitely.[3] There is no doubt of course that we may sometimes have and use paradigmatic instances, somewhat in the way that Victorian school children were taught to use copy-books or the way in which it is convenient to select a carefully measured bronze strip which so long as it is kept at 62^{0} Fahrenheit will be most perfectly a yard long. But the Imperial Yard itself, the type of which this is perhaps indeed the best instance is still a very different matter: it cannot without absurdity be said to vary in length with temperature, or get lost in a fire at Greenwich.[4] In just the sense that its instances may be, it is not a material object.

In what sense would this force us to say that since one may have many instances (copies) of the same poem the poem is not, in the way that they are, a material object? Clearly in some very clear ways it cannot be. For instance, material objects cannot be in two places at once. But, it might be objected, unlike the Imperial Yard, it might well be destroyed or altered in some way. Perhaps if we were to lose all the copies of *Paradise Lost* we would indeed have lost that poem of Milton's. More relevantly for this discussion, poems, in common with all works of art are essentially aretfacts that can be made, brought into existence by their makers doing thing with things. We might press the point harder by asking, as W. Charlton[5] does how indeed we might distinguish type objects in this sense from universals. For just as we can talk of something's being an instance of a certain word, a type of car, the Union Jack, or a named work of art, we may also talk of something's being an instance of the colour red or Hooker's Green. "People want," he says, "to draw the distinction because they want to say that works of art exist and come into being, but not that universals do either, and if works of art are types and types are universals, they will be in a fix. This, however, is only a motive for distinguishing types and universals; reasons are harder to find."

I have to confess that I suffer from a sufficiently low level of metaphysical anxiety for such motives, were they all that was in question, not to be overwhelmingly compelling. If it did seem to me that it would advance our understanding of how we think about colours to suppose that Hooker's Green, the colour, existed and had come into existence in the sense that Hooker's Green, the pigment did, the mere suspicion that this would commit me to an unusual view of universals would not in itself embarrass me very much but this is not so. It is not so in that I do not think that it is very clear what we would be maintaining either way in supposing this, in other words, and this is presumably Charlton's point, it certainly does seem to be the case that the most natural context for the idea of something existing or coming into being is that which applies to coloured things or coloured stuff in a way that contrasts with saying such things about colours themselves. But this is to say very little. It is certainly not to say that there is no clear sense in which something like a piece of music came into existence by being composed, and that what comes into being in this way is not any one of those series of sounds that instantiate it, nor the aggregate of such sounds. The date at which the piece of music, say a symphony, came into being would seem to be the date at which it was composed, not the dates on which it was performed. The date at which the Model T Ford came into being was presumably the date at which it was designed and made in prototype not (and this is a matter of some importance) an easy date to be quite precise about, but not the date at which the individual vehicles rolled off the assembly line. By contrast, it is not at all easy to see what sense could be made of the question when the colour green, or any more precise colour, came into being.

The variety of "universal" which types seem most to resemble, if not to be identical to, is Natural Kinds, such as the Whale, or the Early Iron Age burial mound. For not only can such things have more or less precisely dateable birth- and death-days, we can meaningfully dispute about whether they existed or not. The whale has not existed for ever, and there are many who fear that it may cease to be by becoming extinct, and it would, on the other hand, be perfectly intelligible for an archaeologist to maintain that, while there were indeed early Iron Age burial mounds, there never was such a thing as the Early Iron Age burial mound.

The whale will become extinct when there are no more whales, yet this does not seem to be a good reason for saying that the whale simply is either any particular one or all such animals. To study the whale is not to study all whales: it is to study the characteristics, the normal behaviour of whales, what is essentially, centrally important and interesting about whales. Verbs of interest and enquiry that can be applied to the whale (such as being Jones's obsession) are characteristically opaque with respect to individual whales (no individual whale was an obsession of Jones's). To say of the whale that it has such and such characteristics is not to ascribe those characteristics to any one nor to all individual whales. Similarly, to say that the predator of the wild deer is the wolf, we do not need to be taken as implying that all individual such animals respectively are preyed on by and prey on each other. It is a characteristic of them that they may be standardly inclined to. It is for this sort of reason that someone might well deny the existence of the Early Iron Age burial mound, while admitting that there were burial mounds of early Iron Age people. What would support such a denial is just that there do not seem to be any important ways in which we could isolate the essential features of such mounds in such a way that we could say that without such features, or a significant number of them, a building would not be one of those. The denial would be that we cannot identify a distinct type.

Something may well be an instance of such a type while differing quite markedly from another instance of it, in much the same way as one performance of a given piece of music may still differ quite markedly from another performance of the same music. And this at least distinguishes notions of types in this sense from notions of universals such as the colour green. A given patch of colour can indeed be an instance of a particular colour green but, however wide a band of the colour spectrum that green occupies, it is still the case that such a patch in being such an instance will in that respect be a colour that falls within that spectral band. There need be no question of our distinguishing between the essential features of that colour and the inessential ones. The "abstract objects" that we can identify as types have that characteristic descriptive complexity that permits this which "abstract predicates" such as green (or its somewhat spurious substantive variant, "greenness") lack.

Like natural kinds, such as the whale, or the Round Barrow, which are the objects of text book enquiries and definitions this is often, though not always, the case with type objects such as the Union Jack, or Old Glory. These things, *qua* types, are the objects of a cultural definition that excludes them being either faded or tattered or of any particular size: as types they are simply patterns of a certain sort. We might compare to this an abstract object such as the Euclidian Triangle, of which in so far as it is an object within a mathematical theory cannot be any other way than as it is defined. Triangular fields, on the other hand, while they may very well instantiate, well or less well, such triangles, have as on this account type objects do not have, all the ordinary properties of extended material objects, including colour and location, and also shape. It is the shape they are that permits us to say that they are instances of the type object in question, and if we take to be a logical feature of such shape properties that they might well be a different shape than they happen to be, it will be a consequence of this distinction between type objects and (e.g.) fields that in whatever sense fields can be said to be triangular, Euclidian Triangles cannot be. In the same way, if it is being patterned in a certain way that permits a given piece of cloth to be an instance of the Union Jack, the property of being so patterned cannot in just the same sense be ascribed to the Union Jack itself, *qua* type, for we have rejected the possibility of a type object being an instance of itself.

This consequence is not, it seems to me, objectionable, for it is just what one may have to expect on any account that takes seriously any sort of hierarchy of ontological levels, and there seems to be no reason to suppose that it leads to inconsistencies. What does seem to be the case however is that one cannot consistently both suppose that something such as *The Fifth Symphony* which can be heard at different places at the same time is not to be regarded as logically the same thing as the sequence of sounds that instantiate it and say, as Wollheim does that "anything that can be predicated of a performance of a piece of music can also be predicated of the piece of music itself" (except presumably for its unique location in the concert hall) Charlton's question to him concerning the Union Jack then seems to be perfectly justified, "how precisely does he conceive it? As a rectangular coloured object with no size or place? That sounds very odd." (*ibid.*)

In response to these difficulties concerning types and universals Charlton suggests that we introduce the notion of "possibility" as central.

> The relation of type to token is that of possibility to fulfilment of possibility. . . . The type word "the" is a possible word, and its uses at various points in speech and writing are fulfilments of the possibility . . . so we may say that a piece of music, as contrasted with performances of it, is a possibility. [Hence,] musical composition is thinking up, or working out possible changes in sound. A composer may be said to write down, in musical notation, a piece of music; but what he works out and writes down is strictly a prescription for a performance [by which he tells us that he means] formulae, sets of instructions and directions [for the performance].

His point is that if we think of a piece of music or a work of visual art as a pattern or series of changes in time or in space, we may consider it in two ways "as a type or a token, as a possible change or as the fulfilment of that possibility". If the original distinction between types and their tokens had something of a Platonic ring about it, this way of recasting the matter may well seem to have an agreeably anti-Platonic quality.[6]

And, of course, this takes the matter back to the question of what I have called recipe-following, for this account of a "formula" for a performance corresponds in general to the idea of a recipe. On this account the general issue of what might be called the ontological status of such things as works of art turns out to be part and parcel of the matter of making, in this case the matter of making recipes for artefacts. It also brings together the idea of making a recipe with that of making a design.

Perhaps the most important question one can ask of any philosophical enquiry of this kind is what the pay-off is from the point of view of a less strictly philosophical intellectual enquiry. In terms of this we might well see as more important than any other what may seem to be something of a domestic dispute among the "consensus" of those who have been inclined to extend the idea of types and tokens in this way, namely, whether the account will do for the non-performing arts, in particular for painting and architecture.

A way of putting the matter might be like this. Poems, tunes and those sorts of works of art that are either "made of" words or made to be performed cannot, logically, be bought and sold in the same way as their manuscripts can. One may, of course, hold, sell or buy the copyright in a poem or a song, but one cannot walk off with the poem itself or the song itself, one cannot be the sole owner of the poem, only of the right to reproduce it. There is thus a logical reason why it is not possible to buy up such works of art as a hedge against inflation in the way that one may buy paintings. One may indeed do this with their manuscripts. With paintings the situation is as if they were identical with their own manuscripts. Now the role of the market place in our attitudes to painting and sculpture is of such pressing social importance that it would seem to be more than merely academically interesting to ask whether this is bound to be so and if so why. P. F. Strawson, discussing this topic in *Individuals*[7] is clear enough that this state of affairs is not in any way logically bound to be so. In the case of such things as paintings and most sculpture he argues:

> The things that people buy and sell are particulars. But it is only because of the empirical deficiencies of reproductive techniques that we identify these with the works of art. Were it not for these deficiencies, the original of a painting would have only the interest which belongs to the original manuscript of a poem. Different people could look at exactly the same painting in different places at the same time, just as different people can listen to exactly the same quartet at different times in the same place.

Perhaps the majority of writers who have taken the general view that the distinction between a type object and its tokens can be applied in Aesthetics (for example, Wollheim,[8] Charlton,[9] Wolterstorff,[10] Goodman[11] have in slightly different ways wished to insist that at best pointless and at worst positively misleading when applied to those artefacts and works that are neither performed nor, as poems, novels, and perhaps woodcuts are standardly reproduced. It may make sense to say that I saw the same play in Bristol as you in London, even that I have the same woodcut or engraving in my house as you in yours, but to see the same painting we both have to stand before the same object. Strawson's way of putting the matter seems to perform the logician's trick of taking as a limiting case of a one over many relationship those cases where we have one over one, but if everything that can be predicated of the painting type can be predicated of the predicate token, including its numerical uniqueness, it is easy to see why this can seem to amount to the most empty formalism. One might reply to this on Strawson's behalf, however, that if it is *simply* a technological accident that one cannot at present discern a difference between a painting type and its token, to deny a logical possibility of our ever doing so amounts to a form of special pleading for what may be a passing state of affairs within our culture, that form of special pleadint that consists in "logicing up" a contingency. Seen in this way a dispute of this kind may come to seem to be a version of that fruitless philosophical game that might be called "Who's the Formalist?"

It seems to me however that Strawson is essentially right and that the issue is by no means trivial. We might begin by asking more closely why it is that we cannot, or think that we cannot, grant essential reproducibility in practice, whether or not in principle, to paintings in the way that we manifestly can to poems, and seem to be able to do with engravings and woodcuts. It should be clear that the reason cannot straightforwardly be that we do not have the techniques to make certain that each copy of the original is exactly the same, for no printed copy of a poet's original manuscript is exactly the same as it either in appearance (which is obvious) or in every detail of punctuation, spelling, or even the precise words on the page. Similarly, performances of the same work are not, and are not required to be, identical. It is not, either, a question of the simple amount of departure from some norm that is in question. A performance of a play, say *King*

Lear by an amateur company may involve a very considerable number of fluffed lines, changed or omitted words, even whole speeches and still be accepted as a performance of, withal a bad performance of that play: with all these deficiencies, or departures from some norm that might be exhibited by some favourite excellent performance, we may still be perfectly prepared that it was indeed that play that we saw performed. On the other hand it is more than likely that we would not allow this in the case of a performance that altered really very few lines at the conclusion to give the play, as Nahum Tate's famous production did, a happy ending. Certain departures from the norm are crucial in that they may destroy what we may regard as crucial to our conception of what the play *is*. Certain variations of style and tempo in a musical performance, even a number of wrong notes, are similarly perfectly permissible, others are not; which is a matter of what we conceive the musical work to *be*. And, of course, such conceptions may change. The history of critical interpretation of works of art is in a large part the history of what we, or the critics, in general the cultural environment in which such artefacts exist as identifiable entities, take these things to be. Nahum Tate did not know significantly less of Shakespeare's text than us, the difference lies in how we identify the plays. Certain themes, motifs, aspects of the plays are regarded by us as essential to them that were not so regarded in the eighteenth century. To this extent the text alone[12] (that holy object of literary criticism, the "words on the page") is not, and cannot be, the sole source of what criteria we may have of what counts as the work in question.

This is to say that type objects, such as works of art, are also cultural objects: the context of their identity is common cultural agreement and disagreement. The type object to which that proper name which is the title of the work refers is what encapsulates such criteria of identity (if one likes such terminology, the type encapsulates the criteria of the equivalence class of its instances). This is also why it is possible for most works of art, including most paintings, to sustain considerable peripheral damage, and to survive it. For the distinction between essential and inessential features certainly applies to most paintings. A painting may be rubbed, cracked, even lose quite substantial bits of its surface area and yet survive as that painting that bears the title it has. But not all such damage is peripheral in this way: perhaps in some painting the part of the canvas on which the eyes of a sitter are painted is not so peripheral, or certain glazes or scumbles are not. Disputes about over-cleaning, about, in extreme cases, whether the process of restoration may in fact have been a process of destruction are, just as with disputes over musical or dramatic performances, concerned with disagreements over what counts as being the work of art in question. They are concerned with interpretive judgements of identity. In this case the instances are temporal stages in the history of the material object of which some such stages are accepted as instances of of the type object.

The moral we can draw from this with respect to paintings would then seem to be this, that it is a consequence not only of deficiencies of our reproductive technique that there may be only one instance of any given oil painting, but of our agreement as a critical community that whatever is essential to their being the cultural objects they are cannot carry through a reproductive process. One natural explanation for this may be that we tend to value as essential to the paintings qualities, such as those of texture, variable transparency, even dimension, that we happen not to be able to reproduce satisfactorily. This would still not be a mere technical matter, but at least it would mean that the changes in our attitudes that Strawson envisages would very likely come about with a technical innovation. But this is most unlikely to be the whole story.

A cynical reason why (which might also be the true explanation) might be put down to what I have called elsewhere[13] the "Sotheby Effect", that is to say a vested interest on the part of those who tend by their expertise to form our cultural attitudes to works of art in preserving a way of regarding paintings that conflates their value as works of art with their value as objects of property. In economic terms collecting paintings and collecting postage stamps, or rare books are very much the same sorts of activities. The role of a museum curator, or the director of an art gallery can readily involve a confusion of values. Is he to see himself as the editor of a collection of poetry can see himself, presenting to the public the most worthwhile works of their makers, or as the custodian of a public bank vault, housing the economic treasures of the nation? The uniqueness of a painting that gives it a scarcity value can easily be confused with its unique value as a work of art.[14]

A patron commissioning a unique object of fine workmanship —whether a painting or a piece of furniture—may be to a very large extent paying for not just the aesthetic quality of the work, nor even for the quality of the workmanship, but for its uniqueness *itself*. *That* thing has been made for him, is his and his alone, and no one else can have anything quite like it. Our attitudes to this can be, and perhaps should be, somewhat ambivalent. On the one hand, at, as it were, the top end of the market, we have a case of the mystique of an object of property in the highest degree—the object's value is as an object of property. It is valuable because it is uniquely owned, not owned because, or primarily because, it is valuable. This can easily seem to be a "mystique" because it can, in such cases, seem to be quite irrational, yet as we move from such cases into more humble areas our cynicism may weaken. A dress from a chain store may be as serviceable and as attractive as a bespoke garment, yet a women who values the latter will do so in that its very uniqueness and her possession of it, can help to confirm her as a social individual different from all others. Perhaps we should feel quite confident in scorning such a person for needing to rely on such trivia, for feeling that one we could respect should be able to rely on more serious marks of personality. Yet the desire of individuals to acquire status and dignity in their own eyes and in the eyes of others by the "device" of such unique possession, while a clear source of moral and social silliness and corruption need not in itself be either silly or corrupt. Would the most puritanical of us totally despise someone's wishing to own his own particular bric-à-brac, books or furniture, or a child his own special toys? This role of unique property in establishing a person's moral and social uniqueness is far too basic not to be given a fundamental moral and philosophical respect. It should certainly not be dismissed as mere "bourgeois corruption"; it is too puzzling and too central to our moral experience for that. Yet for that very reason we need to be almost obsessively careful to distinguish that role of objects from their role as "objects of communication". It is the conflict between these two roles that lies at the heart of much of our understanding of the arts in society.

The art historian or scholar who is concerned to establish the pedigree of a painting needs to be clearer than it is sometimes easy to be whether he is concerned to do so in the interest of commerce or in the interest of understanding paintings as the intelligible works of painters. There are possibilities for the corruption of values here that a literary critic, or a music critic may be mercifully free from. To a significant extent the invention of printing has freed our response to literature from these embarrassing ambiguities: it may be instructive to speculate whether things would be different were European poetry "tied" to the calligraphy of its manuscript in the ways that Chinese poetry can be. It can be possible to own a Chinese poem in a way that it is not possible to own the plays of Shakespeare.

In this way it can be tempting to see such graphic art as prints, woodcuts and engravings as a democratic, anti-élitist art form in a way that oil paintings or frescoes cannot be. Since their instances may be owned by many the work of art need not be owned by anyone in particular. This would provide a credible social motive for a painter insisting on adopting such media, and this has sometimes happened. It has, however, rarely happened seriously. Such entirely reproducible works have all too often been produced in limited editions, sometimes for technical reasons in that the reproductive processes may not be accurate over long runs, but clearly also, and quite frankly, to keep the prices high. But the reproductive techniques need not be very difficult. "Minimalist" sculpture, for example, of the sort that may consist in an array of standard units, such as bricks, stacked in precisely describable ways, could surely be reproduced virtually limitlessly: in principle such works need surely have no less sculptural value than an easily printed poem may have poetic value, but what does seem mysterious, and may even be fraudulent, is to attach a price tag to such objects as if they were in principle as unique and hard to reproduce as worked stone.[15] If such works are that good and that easy to reproduce, why are they not as easily available as paperback books? One may imagine an exhibition of "conceptual art" that consists of photographs of, say, landscapes seen in exciting or interesting ways, but what is on sale, the photograph, the "concept", surely not the landscape itself?

These questions are, it seems to me, important, or at all events should be if one supposes both that some valuable sorts of artistic inventions may be involved in such experiments yet at the same time feels that there is something unscrupulous and murky in these matters. A "Strawsonian" view of the matter of reproducibility at least leaves us room for enquiry.

There may, however, be a less cynical explanation for the feeling that works of visual art (what are significantly called sometimes the "plastic arts") have an essential uniqueness that the performing arts may lack, that we should perhaps take seriously. It can be related to the idea of plasticity. If a painting of a drawing is normally identical with its own manuscript, we might well turn the analogy round the other way and say that when someone makes a drawing his activity of composition is identical with a performance of the work. What we look at when we look at a drawing is normally what the maker extemporised, not what he performed. In this respect reproductions of drawing compare to recordings of such things as jazz extemporisations. Although both a drawing and such a musical performance may be to a very considerable extent a development or working up of an earlier sketch, it still remains that in these cases what we hear or see is, as it were, "transparent" to the processes of the object's own making in ways that performances that follow instructions for producing works of a certain type may not be. It should be clear, however, that this difference is one between the performing arts and the non-performing arts, not one between those sorts of works that are essentially reproducible and those that are not, for one *can* hear the very same extemporary musical performance at different places at the same time with the benefit of electronic reproductive techniques. It is interesting, however, that we may still feel that a jazz recording of this sort may still lose something in ways in which recordings of other sorts of music may not, and that this does not have to do entirely with any deficiencies in the equipment: somehow it is as if what may be lost is some more intimate acquaintance with the moment of birth of the work, that it is somehow part of the very idea of that work being the work it is that it belongs to a unique occasion. Moreover, we might feel that the distinction between a fully extemporary performance and the performance of a written work is to some extent a matter of degree. To perform a work is not to follow instructions automatically; in that the instructions do not, and cannot, fully determine how the work should be performed, it is an essential element in the performer's activity that he must interpret the work, that is to say, come to an understanding in performing it what it *is*, what is essential to its being that work. This is, moreover, a simple consequence of what such recipes, instructions and prescriptions are. In that they are recipes, etc. for producing certain types of things they are followed in terms of a degree of systematic contestability concerning what constitutes that type. Even to follow a recipe for making an apple pie is to some degree to come to a conclusion about what is essential to being that sort of apple pie. A performer of a work is thus inevitably to some degree or other also partly a maker, or composer of the work.

One consequence of this is that the maker of a non-performing work has it all his own way when it comes to determining what the work is to a degree that no author or composer of a work that has to be performed can. This is perhaps obvious enough, but it is not the whole story. One motive, perhaps confused and sentimental, but sometimes powerful for all that, that someone may have for valuing the unique material object of the maker's hand (for example the actual paint and canvas of a painting or the manuscript of a poem) can be the feeling that it can somehow put us in touch with the events of his making it in a way that no reproduction of it may, however exact. The material trace of a painter's handling of the paint itself, what is sometimes called "touch", has a peculiar intimacy about it. There can be an excitement in handling a piece of pottery from the remote past impressed with the finger prints of the potter, or in contemplating the very paint surface that Titian handled, or the actual manuscript of a writer's or a composer's composition which is not unlike the sense of having entered a room from which someone important to us has just departed; it is to a degree the excitement of being in something very similar to bodily contact with the agent. We need not approve of such feelings, or regard them as very sensible or justified to understand them, and perhaps most of us share them from time to time. And it will inevitably follow that if we come to regard such things as essential to a response to a certain sort of painting (say) such paintings will not be reproducible. We may even feel that so long as there is any reason to connect the idea of making a work of art with that of inventing a prescription for producing tokens of it, it flies in the face of any common sense understanding of what he did to suppose that he produced a "mere" recipe, for he made a certain unique material object, hence *that* must be the work in question.

However, it by no means follows that those features of an object that, like the imprints of a hand, may show the process of the maker's activity in making it must uniquely belong to the object he handled in so doing. The surface texture of a bronze casting may well do this, but the prints were made in clay not bronze. It would be not merely sentimental but silly to suppose that from the fact that a sculptor's handiwork essentially involved the handling of material that the work he made must be the very material he handled. Similarly, what an engraver handled need not have been the engravings he made, but the block. It is the relatively automatic process of casting and printing that helps to reveal his touch, that printing and casting is a virtually non-interpretive process that can make the prints and casts seem transparent to the physical processes of his making. In no way therefore does it follow that since the sculptor in sculpting is not producing a recipe or a formula he is not making a type object, one which may have, though often does not have, several tokens.

It is very largely in terms of this pattern of thought that there is a tendency to set a value on the hand-made quality of certain works of art and similar artefacts, partly, though not entirely, because they reveal something about the process of their making in their textures. This relates to what is perhaps the simplest and most literal sense of a material having a quality of "plasticity" in that what is plastic can be moulded and shaped at will. The idea of plasticity is of some importance in this context because it has to do with that, not very clear, but quite central, notion of a maker of something expressing what he is after in making it by imposing his will on something else, normally some substance such as clay or wood. The very idea of the plastic arts seems to have to do with this idea of the action of making interacting with such physical and material constraints. Clearly, however, not all uses of the notion of a material's plasticity have to do with what may show the marks of a maker's hand. It is, for example, commonly said that reinforced concrete has this quality, that for example a building such as Lubetkin's Penguin Pool at London Zoo "exploits the plasticity" of concrete. No one would willingly paddle around in setting concrete with bare hands. In this respect no material could be more unlike a sculptor's clay. This may seem to be the merest quibble. What is meant is, of course, that concrete permits a wider range of choices to the designer of the building than does other materials: to say of something that as a material that it has plasticity is to say simply that it can be moulded and shaped at will. The point is, however, that such a material imposes fewer constraints on the designer at the drawing board: it is by no means clear that it can be safely taken to mean any more than that.

The plasticity of concrete as a material for construction refers, for instance, to that property of reinforced concrete to permit a far wider range of choices that may be open to the designer of a building with respect to the shapes he may instruct the builders of it to produce—he can in effect see himself presented with a wider range of options at the planning stage, his constraints in drawing may be less than those presented by more traditional materials. By contrast, in this sense, brick or cob or adobe are less plastic materials. But on the other hand, in contrast to reinforced concrete, these materials may be far more plastic from the point of view of the builders on the site. Although the general constraints on what may be done to produce a stable and successful cob wall may be relatively great in the sense that, for instance, only certain very limited ranges of cross-section can be available to the builder, it can be possible to invent and reinvent the building of such a construction as one goes along in ways that would be quite impossible with a material that requires elaborate shuttering, heavy site machinery and so on. One may imagine a group of workers building a cob cottage for someone's Granny to retire to, responding as they go to her requests and decisions for a window here and an adjustment there in ways that would be in principle impossible for the client of the designers and builders of a more sophisticated construction. Again, such materials as concrete, once set, may be far less easy to adapt and modify later on. In buildings the materials themselves may impose constraints not only on what it may be planned to do, but on the very idea of the construction as a completed finished artefact.

In general, questions about what is made and even who does the making run together with questions about the *constraints* that may be involved at various times and at various ways in the process of a maker's activity. A process of making that tends for quite practical or other reasons to present a greater degree of freedom at the design stage than at the stage of actual construction may well incline us to see the "author" of the artefact as the designer rather than the builder, or, in other contexts, as, to take an extreme example, the poet rather than the printer. A printer, or a building contractor, or the man who stamps out washers we considered in Chapter One, is not the person whose artefact the finished product is in that sense in which the artefact is not the outcome of his thought, intentions and so on. The contractor, the workman or the printer is, we might say, merely carrying out orders, or following prescriptions, not issuing them. In this respect an artefact is something like an intentional object in that it is that thing that someone was making, what he was working on and so on. For to some ineradicable extent "making" and "working on" are psychological verbs whose objects are not simply material stuff that the agent was doing something to, but the objects of the agent's thought. (For reasons I shall be concerned with in the following chapter, however, we should be careful not to simply construe such intentional objects as goals the agent was seeking.) As we saw in Chapter One, the person who stamps out washers is not *working on* what he makes not merely because the process is a relatively fast one, but because what he is doing is not to any degree an expression of thought in what he is making. Conversely, we may sometimes dispute about the identity of the artefact itself in ways that can reveal differences of opinion concerning *whose* processes of thought, or patterns of decision and intention the artefact should be seen as an expression of.

This is perhaps particularly well illustrated in the case of disputes concerning the restoration of old buildings. William Morris, for example, objected to the Victorian "restorers" of medieval churches whose conscious concern was to restore the artefacts, the buildings, to a condition that corresponded as far as could be achieved to the supposed intentions of their original builders and designers. To this end later additions and modifications were stripped away, the mould and moss of time was cleaned and scraped away and where necessary (cynics will say where possible) "Gothic" additions and constructions were added to fulfil the spirit of the original intentions of the builders. It is not quite accidental that the majority of the restorers concerned in this movement were High Anglicans whose interest was to a great extent dominated by an idea of an identifiable original concept of religious building to which it was both possible and desirable to return. William Morris founded the Society for the Protection of Ancient Buildings whose object was, "to keep a watch on old monuments, to protest against all 'restoration' that means more than keeping out wind and weather . . . and to awake a feeling that our ancient buildings are not mere ecclesiastical toys, but are sacred monuments of the nation's growth and hope".[16] To him, such buildings were the products not of some original early designers of buildings but of the communities that nurtured them and used them through the ages. To that extent the two sides of the dispute may be said to have different objects in mind when considering a particular old church, for to restore something is to either mend it or to recover it in all its essentials and the principle behind Morris's objections was that such attempts as restoration were in fact acts of destruction. The buildings were identified in different ways, as a type object may be, by insisting on different essential features. In this case the question of what those features were depended on a view of who should be taken to have made the building, and on how it should be taken to have been made.

What such examples may also indicate is how misleading it may be to see what the maker makes straightforwardly in terms of his intentions or aims in making it. It does on the one hand make fairly straightforward sense to talk of a contractor, or even a performer, acting in accordance with the designer's or the composer's intentions, for the score or the architect's drawing may be said to embody someone's intentions concerning what should be done to construct, or to perform, the artefact he has designed or composed (even if there is at the same time a degree of intended latitude for the contractors or performers). On the other hand someone who in making something modifies, alters, shapes and moulds his material as he constructs it into something cannot so easily be said to be following either his or another's instructions simply, if at all, and cannot very easily be said to be carrying out certain intentions of his or another's. At best we need some vaguer, looser expression than that to be going on with. If it makes sense, as it surely can do, to see the gradual modification of a building such as a village church over the centuries by the accretion of a pattern of decisions, judgements, and intentions of those who had a hand in its being made to be in a certain way, it is at best to force that story into a degree of unnaturalness to suppose that the final outcome was the result of its builders following certain intentions or aims.

And it certainly strains credulity to suppose that such people over the ages acted in accordance with certain formulae as if they were following some plan, only a plan in their heads and not written down. It strains credulity to say this for the point of even supposing that we can sometimes ascribe a kind of corporate authorship to an artefact is that there is thereby a reasonable analogy to an individual maker making something up as he goes along. Extempore performance is not extempore when the performer follows a formula for playing the music, or reciting the poem, even if that formula is in his head and not written down.

This, however, is just what Charlton[17] does want to say.

> "A composer," he says "feels he has done his job when he has written down a formula for others to follow in making instruments sound. The artist does not normally write down a formula to be followed in colouring expanses of canvas or chipping blocks of marble, but himself colours or chips in accordance with his formula."

He wishes to say this because he wishes to recast the notion of a type object in terms of a formula for a range of possibilities while at the same time explaining the apparent collapse of the distinction between types and tokens for the non-performing arts. The resulting picture is then of the maker of such works being, as it were, his own best performer; as he puts it, paintings, statues and buildings are paradigmatic tokens. Following a recipe is, however, not inventing one, and designing or composing something is not following a design or a composition: it is still not following a design or a composition when, which is what seems to be Charlton's thought, the activity of designing or composing issues directly in an artefact that could well have been produced by following a design or composition. What does follow, however, is that so long as such an artefact could well have been so produced it can be in principle reproduced, that it is in other words an "essentially reproducible" type-object.

We can certainly conclude from this that if it makes sense at all to say that a certain artefact can be restored to some condition that preserves its essential features it could be in principle reproduced too: there would seem to be very little difference in principle between the two processes. Someone who felt, for instance, that the newly made stone heads that surround the Sheldonian Theatre in Oxford are adequate restorations of the original will be committed to a claim that amounts, in the terminology of types and their tokens, to saying that new later types have been made of the same token objects. It would seem therefore that to suppose of an artefact, such as a building that one cannot in principle restore it is then tantamount to saying that the process of finally identifying what that object is, in the sense of what its essential as opposed to inessential features are is still unfinished and incompleted. And this is surely just what someone who wishes to maintain something similar to what Morris maintained concerning village churches would wish to be committed to. If such buildings are essentially the continuing products of an historical process, the question of what finally constitutes those buildings in any sense that will provide an answer to one who would seek to restore or reproduce them, cannot be finally and securely answered. The makers of an artefact of this sort have not "done their job".

This may seem to be at best a rather mystical thing to say, but at least some of that appearance can be dispelled if we can avoid the suggestion that to speak in this way is to impute mysterious and unconscious plans and intentions to the community. We need not do this. All that need be supposed is that it may make sense to regard some artefacts of this sort as the material outcome of a process of human agency, and the focus of it. But of course this is a vague thing to say. Can we make it less vague?

We can regard the continuously altered and modified fabric of an artefact such as a village church as having a certain plasticity with respect to the actions and decisions of a community over a period of time in the sense that the material changes in the fabric are able to reflect such actions so that they may even provide clues to such things as the beliefs and attitudes of those who "worked on" the building in this way. To so regard such an artefact is in effect to have made a conceptual decision about it, a decision concerning what it is to count as that building that shows itself in our judgements concerning such questions as when it may be regarded as destroyed or preserved. Disputes between preservationists and restorers whether in the field of architecture or painting, inevitably involve such issues which may be disputable to a greater or lesser extent. In no case can one simply identify such artefacts by "just looking". This is not, of course, to say that one cannot identify the church on the hill or the painting in the long gallery from a picture postcard of it, nor say, what amounts to the same thing that a given picture postcard is a picture of that church that is on the hill or that picture in the long gallery, but these sorts of identifications do not by themselves suffice to resolve disagreements of the sort that importantly do occur between those whose concern it is to understand these objects as the intelligible artefacts of their makers. In such cases the patterns of identification that conform generally to a distinction between a type and its tokens seem inescapable: the several historical stages of such artefacts as they may be altered in time need to be considered as candidates for being instances of the type object in question.

The earlier stages in such a process need not be, even though they often are, paradigmatically best instances. It may be, for instance that a landscape garden, even a building or a painting has been designed to weather and change over time. A "Capability" Brown landscape is perhaps not best instanced by the state of the artefact at that point in time at which the improver's constructive efforts have ceased. Such an artefact in being designed to mature and develop may not be fully exemplified, in the state of best instantiating what it was the maker designed and invented at the time he has finished his job. Just as there may be a question whether the felling of a number of trees destroys or merely modifies such a landscape, so there may equally be a question whether at a stage when those trees were mere saplings the landscape as designed could yet be seen. Similarly, it is at least plausible to suppose a painting designed to change colour with age, to allow for the chemical changes that are normal for oil and varnish. In such a case, it might well be that to restore the picture to a condition similar to that in which it left the studio would be to over-clean it. Whether this was so or not would only partly be a matter of considering the intentions of the picture's maker. What would also be involved might be for example, how we should regard the characteristic style of the period, in general what condition of the picture we might regard as most likely to show to us what we take to be its most characteristic features. (We may, of course, come to think ourselves mistaken in such judgements.) In such cases judgements concerning the various possible and actual states of the picture over time play a role precisely analogous to that played by judgements concerning the appropriate stylistic and other features of a performance. Just as our understanding of the style of a play or a piece of music may determine the latitude with which we are prepared to accept variations of performance as performances of the same work, similar considerations can play a part in the case of the non-performing arts.

This may be in two ways. It is possible for an artefact such as a building, or certain works of sculpture, to be so precisely designed that as designed objects they are quite incapable of sustaining more than the smallest degree of peripheral damage. If it is essential to the design of an object that it should be conceived as, say, a perfectly plain series of precisely placed straight edged solids it may be that the least degree of weathering or staining will have the effect of losing for us just what is essential for the artefact to be seen as an expression of the maker's conception of it: it will cease to be even the paradigmatic, unique, token of that work. Something very much of this sort does seem to be the fate of many buildings of the early movements in modern architecture (e.g. buildings by Mies van der Rohe): the ways that we must see them in order that their design should be intelligible to us makes them aesthetically unstable in that what was once an elegantly placed ordering of space and solidity relying for its impact on the clean lines of its construction (something usually enhanced by making certain that the object is perfectly white) can become, simply through the normal agency of its environment, very close to being a dreary collection of boxes. This is the other end of a scale from how Morris saw his village churches. An important function of decoration, texture, even a certain kind of muddle in the case of artefacts of this sort is thus to make for a certain aesthetic stability. Just as an eighteenth-century landscape may be aesthetically stable over a long period of vicissitudes so may a building of that period. It may still look nearly "right" as a semi ruin.

In a comparable way, general styles of design may be stable or unstable in the sense that one style of design in the arts, whether it be architecture or music, may permit or fail to permit successful use by third-rate practitioners. A style defines types of types. Just as a particular type object may be more or less capable of sustaining "peripheral" damage than another so may a certain style of design be more or less capable of humble and relatively inexpert performance or application than another. Just as too strict an insistence on every feature of a design being essential to its conception will have the effect of a particular artefact being aesthetically unstable—"brittle" might be the most appropriate metaphor—the same may be true of a design-style. Perhaps the most significant virtue of the style of architecture typified by, for instance, Georgian Bath is that it permitted not only the great showpiece terraces and crescents designed by the major architects but also the more humble artisan terraces put up by ordinary builders in a journeyman version of the same style. Such humble buildings were possible not because of any particular excellence on the part of the builders, many of whom were no better than they could get away with, but to the fact that the style they built in was intended for reproduction. This was true in the relatively trivial sense that such builders could have access to ready-made published formulae for, as it were, copy-book houses, but in the less trivial sense that such formulae were based on a relatively clear distinction between what features of a building were essential to its having the style in question and what were not. Generalised "canons" of style do not always cramp good work. Sometimes the effect may be the opposite in that by laying down general principles that clearly are general they both invite, and make room for, invention and modification, sensible adjustment to particular exigencies and so on, in their application. Such general principles become cramping when those who would follow them fail to see them as general, fail to see, as in our earlier example the pedantic cook fails to see, that they need to be interpreted in particular cases and not simply applied by rote. The function of general practical principles of this sort is to enable the practitioner, the maker who follows them, to use his materials intelligently in an intelligible context.

Academism in the arts in the derogatory sense of that word is fundamentally a form of pedantry in practice which, as we have seen, is that intellectual mistake of supposing that principle, recipes, formulae can preempt thought by completely determining what the agent who follows them must do. Academism confuses general principles for doing particular things with particular instructions for doing many different things. An instruction for making washers that determines the outcome in the sense that so long as it is followed every washer will be indistinguishable from another is a "mechanical" principle in just the sense that it determines the outcome as an automatic machine does. General principles for making a certain style of object are not like that. To confuse the two is to confuse the fact that a determinate set of instructions may be repeatable many times over, as a machine for stamping washers may be said to incorporate a principle for "generating" any number of washers, or as the rules for saluting may "generate" any number of salutes, with a practical principle for a type of outcome. Each of these sorts of rules may define a class in the general sense in which they define an equivalence relation. Each individual washer is in a clear sense the "same", e.g., two-inch washer, or each correct salute is "the same" ritual act, but here any distinction between essential features and inessential features of such things has become vanishingly unimportant or irrelvant: in such cases to apply the principles is typically not to be required to think. Washers are not essentially reproducible in the sense which began this chapter, like salutes, they are reproducible *tout court*. Principles for producing type objects, or conceptions for identifying them are not concerned with reproduction *tout court*. Either way they are interpretive.

If academism is the characteristic fault, like moral pedantry, which makes general practical principles over-determinate, there can be a form of reaction to it which errs in the reverse direction, yet makes a similar assumption. European and American thinking about the arts in the present century has been particularly anxious to avoid the crippling conventionalism so often associated with the very idea of canons of good practice both from the point of view of the makers of works and their interpreters. The ideal of the free spirit of the creative artist who makes something new unconstrained by general conceptions and principles has during much of this time been the dominant one. Hampshire's contrast[18] between the world of the arts which is not, and the world of morals which is concerned with what is "essentially general" is in all sorts of ways typical of this reaction. In many ways it is a view of the maker and his task that appeals to the Romantic ideal of the artist as an isolated Promethian genius, with the idea that the outstanding creative artist is not different in degree, but in some not very clear way in kind, from the general run of those who do the best they can. What he makes, if successful is unique, is ungeneralisable. In terms of a maker's design this can have the consequence of supposing that so long as what he has designed has succeeded, and to the extent that it has, its virtues are unique and peculiar to it. In painting this means that every brush stroke, every discernible aspect of it becomes essential to its being that particular object of value and a similar view applied to an object such as a building that has to be designed on paper would have it that *just* those arrangements of shapes and volumes, just those details and proportions etc are what constitutes whatever peculiar excellence it may have. In practice nobody could quite suppose this, but so long as the feeling somehow lurks in the background that such an ideal of uniqueness ought in some way to apply there is likely to be a reduced incentive to look for what in general should be retained in (say) a battle over a building, or what in general should be, or could be, learnt from a successful artefact. The notion that the best is somehow perfect in this sense is unlikely to encourage anyone to look for a way of achieving the best within the limits of modest, humble attainment, for the very idea of doing so will seem to involve a contradiction in terms. The price of insisting on nothing but the best may if the "best" is seen in this way, leave us with nothing. It may certainly leave us with a bewildering gap between excellence and total mediocrity. This is by no means the only explanation of why it is that the present century has produced few buildings comparable with the humbler products of the past, but it seems inescapable that such a way of thinking has played too great a part. Like academism, it assumes an over determinate role for practical principles.

It is no accident that the same critical movement that stressed the place of the idea of the identity of certain artefacts such as buildings within a context of social process should at the same time have seen it important to insist on the place of the "hand-made" in design. The "arts and crafts" movement associated with William Morris was all of a piece with the principles of The Society for the Protection of Ancient Buildings popularly known as "Anti-Scrape". Partly, and perhaps most importantly, this was for overt political reasons. Put at their crudest, they amount to a view that the most valued artefacts in our environment should somehow be the expression of the practical imagination of ordinary people skilled in the discipline of handling materials. But expressed in this way such a view is at best sentimental and utopian in the worst sense. Many of the things we need simply cannot be well made by hand, any more than it is possible, let alone desirable, to leave the final conception of an object such as a bridge to be worked out in the making of it. It is hard to see how any sort of a society, let alone a socially just one, could fulfil the needs of present-day people on the basis of hand-made objects. Yet we can still abstract from the somewhat sentimental context of that tradition of thought about made things and those who make them—which is responsible at the worst for that rather sickening preference that certain people will show for the most inconvenient and expensive hand-made pottery, fabric, etc. over any other mass-produced alternative, a form of silliness that Morris and his followers should not be blamed for—and identify an important observation concerning the nature of the intelligent process of making. It can be a tempting thing to say that a maker who finds out how to make something finds out how to achieve some end which he has set himself, attempting to bring into being something of which he has a clear conception, while lacking at most the knowledge of how to achieve it. The temptation is to say that the rationale of a maker's activity depends on the concept of the object he is seeking to make. But this simple means-end picture will not always fit the facts. It especially will not fit the facts of a maker's activity where he is not following a prescription for using his materials, but using his materials in "discovering" what it is that he is making. But this has nothing especially to do with what is hand-made even though it may seem best shown in cases of this sort of making. To see what it has to do with it will be necessary to examine a little more closely the notion of a goal.

To say that a work of art is a type-object is to say that our understanding of what it is, what makes that particular material object, collection of sounds, marks on paper and so on, either uniquely, or together with other things *count* as that work, that object that bears the title, is to say that it is the object of a particular sort of understanding. It is to see it as a designed whole. Critical disputes, and interpretive disputes have to do with what the observers, the public, the audience take the object to be and the conditions of their understanding. There will be parallel questions for the maker himself. What does he take himself to be doing, even, what does he take himself to be making?

Notes

1 Nicholas Wolterstorff, "Towards an Ontology of Art Works", *Noûs*, Vol. IX, No. 2, May 1975.
2 When I read a paper on this topic with the title "Works of Art and Other Cultural Objects", *Proc. Aristotelian Society*, Vol. XX, January 1968, it was objected to me that the title had a certain similarity to "Helen of Troy and Other Women"—we all know Helen was female but that is not what makes her special. Still, she was a special *woman* and it was that which made her special.
3 There is an obvious parallel between this regress and Plato's so-called Third Man argument in the Parmenedes the upshot of which is that we should not regard forms as *resembling* their instances. cf. *Parmenedes* 133, and my "Works of Art and Other Cultural Objects" pp. 111 ff.
4 cf. Colin Strang, "Plato and the Third Man", *Proc. Aristotelian Society*, Sup. Vol., 1963. (The example here is Strang's.)
5 W. Charlton, *Aesthetics*, Hutchinson University Library, 1970.
6 In my earlier discussion of this (*op. cit.*) I referred to myself as a Platonist of the Nominalist persuasion. There is a certain metaphysical embarrassment attached to the matter. Partly it may be for this reason Goodman in his in many ways, seminal discussion of the problem of the identity of art works prefers to avoid a type-token basis for the account to "dismiss the type altogether and treat the so-called tokens of a type as replicas of one another",

cf. Nelson Goodman, *Languages of Art*, Oxford University Press, 1969, p. 131. Goodman prefers instead to base his account on a distinction between what he calls "autographic" and "allographic" works, where the former have and the latter do not have what might be called "manuscript status". The effect of this, as the title of his book indicates, is to centre the discussion on the intrinsically fascinating issue of notations for the performance and replication of art works rather than on what is for me the slightly wider issue of their reproducibility and preservation. Both types of approach have it in common that they depend on taking works of art and design seriously as artefacts of communication. Where they tend to differ is over the question of how deeply embedded in the logic of the system of analysis we give should be the requirement that e.g. a painting's identity should depend on its being the product of its painter's hand. Another way of putting that matter can be that it has to do with the *level* of the explanation we give of the fact that a painting can be forged whereas a poem cannot.

7 cf. P. F. Strawson *Individuals,* Methuen, 1959, p. 231 fn.

8 cf. R. Wollheim, *Art and its Objects.*

9 cf. W. Charlton, *Aesthetics.*

10 *op. cit.*

11 cf. Nelson Goodman, *Languages of Art.*

12 Unless we extend the notion of text out of all normal limits.

13 cf. "Works of Art and Other Cultural Objects".

14 A writer in the *Guardian* investment advice section (April 10 1976) said, "Satisfactory art investment requires a delicate balance between a feeling for beauty and a need for profit. A healthy appreciation—in both senses of the word—is the name of the game." It would be hard to find a more unhealthy confusion than that between the two senses of that word. Unhealthy, for an understanding of the arts, that is.

15 cf. The furore during Spring 1976 over the Tate Gallery's purchase of a Carl André sculpture for an undisclosed (but supposedly large) sum.

16 *The Political Writings of William Morris,* ed. A. L. Morton, Lawrence and Wishart, 1973, p. 16.

17 *op. cit.,* p. 33.

18 *loc. cit.*

CHAPTER FIVE

DESIGNING WHILE MAKING

To justify a course of action as a means to a certain end presupposes that one has some adequate knowledge of what end it is that one is seeking. However subtly a recipe may need to be interpreted in the light of an understanding of the conditions of its application a recipe is still a recipe for achieving something. To follow a recipe successfully is to achieve what it is a recipe for. Certainly not all practical principles are concerned with achieving certain ends; as we have seen, a principle that states the right thing to do on a given occasion (for instance a rule of etiquette) is not. But then, such principles are not, it would equally seem principles for getting things done, certainly not for getting things done in the sense that to make something is to get something done. It would seem to be obvious enough that to complete the task of making something, to bring the process to a successful conclusion such that one can say that what one is engaged in making is finished, *must* be to have reached some goal that one has set before one. I will have finished the business of making a chair, or a pie, when there is just such a chair or pie as a result of my actions. Surely, I can only be significantly said to have been successful in the matter so long as that was in fact what I *was* trying to achieve. It would also seem to be obvious that a condition of being able to report that I was trying to achieve such an end must be that at some earlier time I set out to do so, that, at some earlier time I *could have said* that it was a chair or a pie that I was trying to make, that, in other words, I knew what it was I wanted.

Conversely, it seems to count quite naturally against the rationality of a person's actions—or course of activity—that he has no very clear idea what it is that he does want. It counts against his rationality to say this because unless we can say this of him we cannot give a rational account of what it is that he is doing. To describe someone as making a chair differs from, for example, saying that he is running in that we incorporate into the description a reference of what it is that he wants to achieve: "he is making a chair" in this sense means much the same as "he is trying to make a chair" (perhaps not quite, for if we suppose his attempts to be *quite* hopeless we will probably not say that he is *making* a chair) and a way of accounting for this can be to say that in so describing his actions we are giving his rationale. It can equally seem that to offer such rationale-giving accounts is paradigmatic of what it is to fulfil an essential condition for our being able to say that his behaviour is rational. It permits us to say that his behaviour is intentional, that it is purposive, that he has reasons for doing what he does and for failing to do other things, otherwise his activity will not be a candidate for rational assessment. How can we say any of these things if he does not know what he wants, for these things have to do with success and failure, and if he fails to know that how could he know whether or not he has been successful in what he does? This is the orthodox picture.

Accordingly, let us imagine a painter's studio. Round the walls there may be a variety of paintings, some successfully completed, others not yet completed to which certain things have to be done in order that they should be finished, and yet others, perhaps, that have been left unfinished by the painter and set aside because he has no very clear idea what to do with them next. There may be others that have got started but have so clearly gone wrong that they have been abandoned altogether. Clearly, if we or he can classify these things in any of these ways he or we must have some understanding of what is meant by success or failure in activities of this sort.

Suppose that we talk to him about his work in order to learn from him what lies behind this understanding. To do so is to find out something of what it is to paint. Why, we ask, does he do this, why that? Like the wall builder he may respond by telling us that certain things are done in order to achieve certain effects, that conversely, if one wants to achieve certain effects certain things have to be done. He may even, if we are good, tell us why this is so. Like the wall builder, he tells us certain recipes for achieving one thing and another, and, like the wall builder he may sometimes show us that what he has said can only be understood in terms of an understanding of how the materials behave. But he is not quite like the wall builder for all that. We know of the wall builder that he wants the wall to lie across the ground in a certain direction at a certain height and to have a certain degree of strength and solidity. We do know just what he is trying to achieve. What we do not know, perhaps, is how he achieves it. Accordingly, we ask the painter what he is trying to achieve. How, we ask, does he hope that the finished picture will be? When the picture is successfully completed, what we ask, will it be like? The painter cannot tell us that, however. He may even say that were he to know that there would be little point in his painting the thing, for the interest for him in his doing so consists to a large extent in his finding that out. But then, how does he know when he has finished? Does he even know what it is that he is trying to do? And if he does not, how can we say that his activity has a rationale, is purposive, intentional, even rational, and so on. Of course, we may say that his activity is creative, and that creative activity *is* if not irrational, at least non-rational. But need we conclude this?

How real a philosophical problem does this present, and if real how general? We need not have taken a painter as our example. Many sorts of makers would do as well—even writers of essays in philosophy. Does a writer of an essay know right through his activity of composing his thoughts on paper how the thing, if at all successful, will finish up? There will, of course be times, and he may be happier if such times become more frequent while he progresses, when he may have a pretty good idea how the final version will go. But, unless he is merely reporting something that he has already worked out, at best such times will be more or less clear glimmerings of the final result that he is after. To work something out whether in words on paper, paint on canvas, or in any other medium, is in a very important sense to discover something, to discover what will satisfy the maker of the artefact. Even when a writer is concerned with the final polishing of the final draft of what he has written when he begins his polishing he will not be able to tell himself or others just how the words will stand on the page. Being able to do that is what he is after. To a considerable extent writing the words on the page *is* his way of finding that out. His final draft is not a *report* of how the words will stand, for writing it is *making* them stand just so. If he could report in advance just what the final result of his efforts will be, having completed the task, that report itself would be the completion of his task and writing it would be undertaking it. A painter can only show himself and others what, if successful, his completed picture will be like by showing himself and others the picture completed. That is what it *is* to compose something.

Does it follow from this that the composer of something has no goal, that he does not know while engaged in his activity what he is after, and even then would it follow that his activity is thereby not a rational one or has no clear rationale? It might be argued that none of this follows.

In the first place it is simply not true that the painter or the writer has *no* goals before him when he sets out on his project or as he continues with it. At least he wants to paint a picture, or to write a paper, and a good one. Almost certainly he wants to paint a picture of a certain sort, or to write a paper on a certain topic, often a picture of a very specific sort or a paper on a very specific topic. He may, moreover, have very clear criteria of what would make a picture of that sort, or a paper on that topic a good one, even if he necessarily cannot describe what the particular painting or paper will be like when it is finished. He may "have his standards", and to have such standards is, among other things, to have good enough criteria of what it is that may count as a good result of the kind he seeks. Surely, these are just the sort of considerations that do constitute his goals. Only when they fail to apply can we say that he has no idea what it is that he is trying to do. Surely, we indicate as much by reporting that what he is doing is painting a picture of a certain kind or writing a paper on a certain topic. Is that not precisely to offer a goal- or intention-based account of what he is doing?

We might reinforce such a reply by repeating what has been said earlier, namely, that it is a mistake to suppose that general practical principles for doing something should be construed as specific instructions for performing precisely determined actions. Similarly, the same sort of mistake would be involved in supposing that an intention, aim, or goal must involve an agent's ability to give a unique description of what may, if he is successful, fulfil his intentions. It may, of course be that someone may want a particular thing in the sense that he will accept not just anything of a certain kind, but *that* book or to meet that particular person. But equally obviously someone may want to meet a pretty girl, or to explore a beautiful landscape without knowing, even without very much caring, just what particular girl or place would satisfy him. In general the idea of an agent's knowing what he wants requires only that he should be able to give some account of what would satisfy him in the sense that he can give some description of what would count as a successful completion of the project he is engaged in. It makes no difference to this general notion of *knowing what one wants* whether that description is very precise or not, whether it is, for instance meeting a pretty girl or meeting Mary Jane. In this sense the idea of an agent's having a goal would seem to be just as accommodating as the general idea of being able to describe a situation in which he may find himself. Not being able to describe in detail *just* how the picture he is engaged in painting will, if he is successful, turn out to be like would thus seem in no way to warrant our saying that the painter's activity is not goal-directed.

Yet, still, there is something about his situation that does seem to be odd so long as we regard what he is doing in terms of purposeful, goal-directed activity. The difficulty does not have to do with the idea of a goal simply, but with that of a goal-directed activity. As we have seen, that idea has built into it the conception of the agent's rationale, his "thought in what he is doing" being capable of being exhibited in terms of his being able to justify what he does as means to the ends he seeks. Very clearly this is to an *extent* true of the activity of the painter or the writer. His work is a means to the end of producing a good painting of a certain kind, or a paper on a certain topic. But this will only take us so far, and sometimes so far as that it is not far enough. We might express this by saying that such intentions constitute *minimal ends,* "minimal" in that they offer a minimal account of what he is after. Other such "minimal ends" might be such things as wanting to lead a good life—it is *something* to aim at, but we can say little more than that.

It seems obvious enough that if a painter's purpose in painting, or a composer's in composing, or a writer's in writing is to produce a satisfactorily completed painting, piece of music or paper, an essential condition of our being able to make sense of what he is doing in purposive terms should be that we can give an account of his recognising that he has successfully completed the job in hand. This is easy to do in a simple case of someone trying to hit a haystack at five paces: when whatever he is trying to hit the haystack with at that distance is successfully lodged there from where it is projected he has achieved what he is trying to do. If Spotty Fred wants to get Mary Jane, or just any pretty girl, into bed with him he knows well enough before he sets out that the situation of being in bed with Mary Jane, or with some pretty girl, will count as a successful end to his endeavours. We may doubt that even the simplest souls could have such simple aims, but what we need have no difficulty about is how, given such ambitions, they can recognise their fulfilment. However hard it may be to imagine how Spotty Fred can achieve his amorous designs, however lacking in perception he may be, even he is hardly doing anything mysterious in recognising that at last there he is, just as he had always hoped. But what does the writer, or the painter or composer recognise? There is no doubt that he must recognise something.

Confined to aesthetics such a question as this can easily seem to be the same one as what criterion we may have as to what counts as a good work of art of a certain kind—a topic in a theory of criticism. (Presumably a parallel question in a case where the artefact is a philosophical paper would be a topic in a theory of philosophical criticism.) The issue clearly has to do with such questions but it is not confined to them. Our question is how does the *maker* of the artefact recognise that his work is done, that the thing is made? And just as the idea of a goal is integral with that of a purposeful course of action, so this question is integral with the very idea of a maker's activity in making.

Quite idle activity may in a minimal, but not totally insignificant sense, be said to have a purpose. Someone who doodles to pass the time in a committee, or who idly makes patterns of pebbles and sticks while sun-bathing has *some* purpose in what he does—that of passing the time by doodling or pottering. One way of saying, however, that his activity is aimless is that he does not set out to make anything in doing this. He does not even set out to make a doodle. But someone else might do just this. His aimless doodling may even take him over so that he becomes absorbed in his doodle, concentrates on it, on the shapes he is making, so that he finds that he is concerned with making a design. He is then half-way to designing something. Then what he is doing is not aimless, absent-minded, abstracted, but becomes intent and absorbed. This can be something to avoid in a committee, for the business may then pass him by along with the time. However, though what he is doing may become less aimless it need not follow at all that he has any more of an idea of what it is that he wants to achieve: he is concentrating on making a design, but he is not concentrating on an activity which he sees as a means to the end of producing a design. What he is concentrating on is the design he is making, what he is doing, not on something that can, he hopes, lead to what he has not yet done, even though he may hope to finish the job he is engaged in.

Designs and purposes are related, but they are clearly not the same thing. To do something designedly, or by design, does, more or less as far as such idioms may be relied on, mean much the same as doing something on purpose and sometimes even *for* some purpose. To accuse someone of standing on one's foot on purpose does not mean that he had some purpose that he wished to achieve by standing on one's foot, only that he meant to stand on one's foot, that it was no accident or mistake. To do something designedly often means not more than that: it is often a rather old fashioned way of saying that it was done on purpose. On the other hand, to do something *for* a purpose is normally to do something as a means to some further end. Similarly, to do something as part of a design seems to be a slightly old fashioned way of saying the same thing. Ambiguities of this sort have caused trouble in philosophical contexts. The idea of design is sometimes talked about as if it were integral with the idea of purposes or ends (as if it was always related to Spotty Fred having designs on Mary Jane). In fact it has to do with the much more general idea of something being ordered.[1] It is sometimes supposed, for instance that the very idea of the world as a whole having a design must imply that it is supposed to fulfil some purpose, perhaps God's. The so-called "argument from design" is often supposed to have built into it the idea that to suppose that God designed the world He must have done so, not merely on purpose, that is to say, not in a moment of divine inadvertency, but for a purpose, to fulfil an end. All that need be meant, which is mystical enough in all conscience, is that He designed the world, that is to say that He gave it some order with the theological implication that in doing so He expressed some thought in the design. The idea of God as an architect does have transcendental implications, but the implications are to the world having a significance, being "the book of the world", not, as is often supposed, that of serving some end.

To talk, for example, of the design of a clock, or a system—something that works in a certain way, need not even have these implications of indicating the thought of its maker, though, of course so long as we suppose that it was made and designed we may if we wish study it as a clue to that thought. It can be enough that we can see the parts articulated in a certain way, that we can see, as it were, that thus and thus is how it works, for when it works these parts do this and that in connection with each other. We can, in other words, see how the parts function in terms of the inter-relations of the thing as a whole. If a clock were to come into existence ready made, not made by any designer, we could still say that, could still investigate its design in the sense of how its parts function. It is sometimes supposed that functional explanations of this sort (or comparable explanations in biology) must have "teleological" implications, must entail assumptions and conclusions concerning ends and purposes. They need not. It might be less disastrous to suppose that they have overtones of something's expressing thought, but they need not have these overtones either. The implications are, rather, to the idea of something's being intelligible in terms of how its parts are ordered and inter-relate in terms of the whole of which they are parts. To design something, on the barest account to make a design, is to be concerned with making something in this way. The activity of making a design is not the activity of doing something for a purpose.

However, to do something for a purpose, to achieve or bring about some end is to do something which is, in a relatively straight-forward sense, a part of a whole (it is to do something which is a component of a total policy, and which can be understood as such). It would seem, therefore, that doing something for a purpose is a species of designing—a fact that we seem to pay tribute to when we say that Fred has designs on Mary, or that his buying her chocolates is part of his design, that he does so designedly. It is naturally assumed that to understand an activity, or course of action, can be to see it as a component in a plan or policy, as a means to some end, but these reflections would suggest that such a way of understanding actions is merely a species of a more general way, that the more primitive idea of an intelligible activity has to do with that of designing.

Can we find an example of a course of action that is as it were "all designing" with the minimum amount of end-seeking? How far might we go in finding such a course of action intelligible? If we were to call this sort of thing free invention, what will it be free of?

Such an example might well be provided by considering that sort of painting that is often called "Action Painting", the implication of that expression being that in that sort of free abstract painting what is communicated to the observer of the completed artefact is, as well as a beautiful and fascinating pattern of paint and colour, a record, or expression of, the activity of the painter in painting it. Clearly, to some extent, any paint surface can show in its "touch" and the way in which the paint has been handled, something of this. As we have seen, it is the feeling that this is so that can provide one aspect of the excitement and interest of any painting, and of many other hand-made artefacts, but in the case of this sort of work it is as if this aspect has been isolated to the exclusion of virtually all else.

The history of stylistic change in the plastic arts in this century is to a large extent the history of successive attempts to isolate aspects of what in an earlier time would have been regarded as an essentially complex matter. It can be well worth asking why, for the most natural explanation is one that pays tribute to the general idea of an artefact—especially one of this sort—being an analysable form of communication. A well-intentioned, relatively un-Philistine observer of the passing scene in the world of the so-called fine arts might be forgiven a certain cynicism in the face of the rapidity of changes in stylistic fashion in the present century. Action painting itself is, after all, long out of style by the time-scale of this process. At the start of the century it seemed to most sensitive and intelligent observers of the arts that the set conventions and expectations concerning what the arts ought to be, and in particular how painting ought to be, so inhibited the very possibility of creativity and invention, and above all of saying or doing anything serious and worth while, that at all costs it was necessary to break the mould of such conventional expectations. The slogan "make it new" that writers such as Ezra Pound and others coined for the role of the creative artist was a response to this. But the idea of originality, of doing something new, the idea of creativity and invention, and that of being able to produce a shock effect against the expectations of the academic and the conventional, are three ideas that are by no means identical. In the early years of this century they could easily be seen so, and they have tended to be confused with each other during subsequent decades. To begin to make headway in understanding the nature of inventive thought in making things it is necessary to be on one's guard against such conflations, and for this it can help to ask why, that is to say in reaction to what, they could come to seem natural and inevitable. The question has a great deal to do with coming to understand the point of any stylistic departure.

Perhaps most people think they have a fair idea what they would mean by a conventional academic painting, or a conventional response to painting: for many it is still summed up in the word "Victorian" even though it is by now far less clear than it used to be that all the official respectable art against which new generations reacted was inevitably second rate. It is, however, doubtful whether even those who know the detailed history of the period of rebellion against "the conventional" at the start of this century would call to mind the same painting, or the same sort of paintings as typical artefacts of "the enemy". For "academism" in the sense that has to do with the history of the arts, and of what might be called stylistic struggle, is not an expression that should be taken as identifying any particular style at all. To suppose that it refers to a way of painting, for instance in the manner of the Royal Academy at a certain date, the French Salon at another, or even that currently regarded as respectable by the official establishment of the Soviet Union, would be a mistake. If the term has any meaning it should be seen as having to do with a particular attitude to the role of artists, and other makers of artefacts as providers of things that other people value. Perhaps above all it is an attitude to "Art" with a capital "A", an attitude that it is something both worth having and reassuring that fulfils a peculiar social function, that of providing an alibi for the imagination. Just as a certain sort of regular church- or chapel-goer could, in the days when such activities were more fashionable than they are now, reassure himself that he was concerned with "morality" by that simple social performance, and thus feel relatively untroubled by particular moral issues, or by moral issues outside his familiar experience, so the person of "taste" may find himself reassured by his regard for Art to the extent that he need feel little pressure on him to exercise his imagination outside the range of what is familiar to him. The two phenomena are closely related as part of a general pattern of a recognisable sort of complacency. Naturally enough, leaders of society who have, for one reason or another, been inclined to value a quiet life for themselves, tended to be in favour of such institutionalised attitudes and of others like them.

By the close of the nineteenth century the most familiar sort of painting tended to be that which was fairly straightforwardly representational in terms of the representational conventions most commonly associated with oil painting, and certain sorts of subject matter had tended to become regarded as more natural than others as fitting for such treatment. Accordingly, when we look back on that period we tend to think of conventional, academic, styles of painting in these terms. But that we do so is very largely an historical matter. In the past, portraits or history painting, in the Grand Manner, in our own time Social Realism, and perhaps at an earlier period quite different styles of religious painting, have all fulfilled the same sort of rôle.

In reaction to this there was no doubt that, at the start of this century, it was necessary to shock the complacent and the conventional lovers of Art out of their preconceptions if the observers of what the makers of paintings were concerned with were to be deprived of their excuses for not paying attention to what was put before them. To achieve anything it was thus necessary for the artist to shock, to break the mould of the familiar; originality in this somewhat specific sense became identified with any kind of creative success. At the present time, however, a cynical (not necessarily a Philistine) reaction to the state of the arts, especially the visual arts, might well be forgiven for seeing the very insistence on originality, on the need to reform the very idea of what painting is every few years, as a new kind of conformism of the imagination, the institutionalising of revolutionaries of the imagination as mere entertainers. In this manner he might see that just as one gallery may make its money by dealing in the gilt-edged securities of the familiar past, others, "contemporary" galleries, are concerned with the fashion trade: the very word "contemporary" has acquired very much this sense in our language. It is the phenomenon of property, and of reassuring property at that. Newness can be a commodity like any other.

But the cynic would, in supposing that this is the whole explanation for the rapidity of stylistic change in this area, be only half right. Behind such a cynical parody of the situation lies a not altogether clear, but still important, assumption that activities such as painting, and artefacts such as paintings have to do with communication. The sense in which this is so is not at all easy to define, but if we assume that it has some sense we can perhaps offer a slightly different account of the matter. If we take the familiar, conventional style of oil painting at the start of his parody of history, as a starting point, it is not very difficult to see that to respond to such an object with even the beginnings of a serious understanding, it is necessary to pay attention to several quite different aspects of the object in several quite different ways and to then orchestrate those responses. This need not be done very consciously, though it can be, and in the case of a complex and difficult painting perhaps has to be. Such a picture is the representation on a flat surface of objects to which we, and we assume the painter, may adopt, or have adopted, certain attitudes. These objects may be placed in certain ways as in a dramatic presentation, so we are invited to see them thus and thus in relation to ourselves and to each other. Their inter-relations may be symbolic in more or less conventional ways, or they may illustrate, or even tell, a story. The masses and groupings of colour and shapes may interest us or be disturbing to us, and thus invite us to pay attention to ways of seeing colours and shapes in ways we may not have hitherto suspected. The ways in which the painter has handled the materials he has used, how he has spread the paint itself may have its own significance. Even the ways he has used and modified the conventions of representation may need to be noticed, for it may play a part in how the picture is to be seen, how it works on us. This is a complex matter, even if to remark on it as briefly as this is to say nothing very new or surprising. In some sense, even if an obscure and unclear sense, it is as if this sort of complex of responses, and the possibility of them is, as it were, the "grammar" of the possibility of such an artefact's being able to communicate something—these possibilities are the conditions of being able to *understand* the picture. On the whole, theorists of the idea of understanding and communication—such as philosophers—though they have paid much attention to these things in other areas, have paid little attention to these sorts of understanding or to these sorts of communication. Any analysis of such conditions has inevitably had to be done by the painters (and perhaps their critics) themselves.

To a great extent this is the general challenge that painters seem to have responded to in this century. It is as if the question were constantly being asked how far can one go while restricting the exercise to one, or virtually one, of these aspects of the "original" whole. The question has not been asked like that, however. Indeed, it is often not so much asked as begged systematically. From time to time painters and their critics have claimed that *this* or *that* way of seeing a picture is the only serious way. We have been told, for example, that to be interested in what the objects depicted are, what they represent for us, what moral or other value they have, is to show a spurious "literary" interest in the picture, that representation is all ("sit like an apple," said Cézanne to his wife, "does an apple move?"). At other times it has been as if the ways in which the painter has handled forms and colours, and that alone, has been the name of the game; at others the exploration of methods of representation on a flat surface, and the relation of that surface to the space of the represented objects has been the central concern; at other times, as with certain sorts of Dada or Surrealism, how we regard the objects, our conventional and less conventional attitudes to them and assumptions about them has been what the painter has had to do with (the point, to take a hackneyed example, of putting a urinal on a plinth, is to a very considerable extent that people do not expect such a thing to be that respectable object, a piece of sculpture: were we to get more used to the idea of such objects being in art galleries rather than at the back of public houses, that Dada effect would vanish—this *is* in effect a "literary" use of the artefact). Seen in this way, which is of course not the whole story, the succession of styles is a, albeit experimental and rough and ready, process of analysis of the phenomena of the intelligibility of made things. Action Painting can be seen as isolating the aspect of the "touch" of a picture, its capacity to bear witness to the maker's actions in making it. This is not, of course, to say that it may be central to the importance of such an exercise that the objects thereby produced should be lovely to look at: it is however, to say that so long as the exercise is serious the loveliness should be of a kind that has to do with this capacity.

When this sort of painting became fashionable the uninitiated and impatient, who are not always perfectly silly, even if some may be, reacted in effect by saying that though the canvases of (say) Jackson Pollock were delightful enough to look at as "mere patterns" how could there really be a difference between what he was doing in making them and simply doodling? This was the right question. It seemed, however, to be the right question for the wrong reasons. Dribbling, pouring, splattering paint all over large sheets of canvas ("even riding a bicycle over the thing! Whatever next!" was the conventional exclamation) hardly seemed to serious people to be serious work. Couldn't anyone do that? Such questions invited the wrong response which was to reply, in effect, that so long as someone as good at doodling as the best painters of this sort doodled, and so long as the result was good to look at, what matter? But the question may be serious (just as each breakaway stylistic episode has been able to invite similar serious questions, even from the Philistines) for it assumes a general question which is what in any case is the difference between doodling and designing when the latter is done in the freest possible way?

Let us imagine a very thinly described story of someone making such a pattern and being serious and intent about the matter. In some way doodling is not similarly serious and intent, so perhaps we may be able to identify what that difference really amounts to. Such a question is ultimately a question in the philosophy of action. (My speculative interlude into a parodied history of twentieth-century art is to suggest that such philosophical questions may sometimes be asked practically.)

We can substitute such a practical enquiry by imagining a somewhat simplified thought-experiment. As with all such thought-experiments it involves a considerable, even a gross, simplification but that is, of course, one of the virtues of such an exercise. Let us imagine someone who, equipped with paint and canvas, sets himself the minimal aim of producing a pattern that delights, or satisfies him as far as possible. We can call this a minimal aim for the natural reason that while such an ambition *is* a goal of sorts, what achieving such a goal might amount to could hardly be inferred from such a description. About all we might infer (and perhaps even this might be rash) is that somehow or other the paint has to finish up on the canvas, but such a description of a possible state of affairs does not even give any information about what sorts of situations might delight him, or satisfy him, it does not even give us any information about any possible difference there might be between his being delighted by his result or merely satisfied by it. On the other hand, there seems to be no reason why such a minimal aim should be unintelligible. It is a possible thing to want to do. In so far as it is not unintelligible, we may therefore suppose that the agent himself knows very little more about what he is aiming at than we can infer from such an account: it represents all that he can at this stage say. There does, however, seem to be just one thing more that we can infer from his having such a minimal aim, namely, that he is interested in trying to *find out* what might fulfil it.

He can approach this goal in the following way. At first he can make a mark on the canvas with a more or less random smear, or splurge of paint which he may then attend to. He may either be quite indifferent to the situation he has produced, or dislike it to some degree, or like it to some degree. It is not necessary for him to have such a response to what he has done for him to know why he reacts in the way that he does. If that mark is a purplish shape of one sort or another there may be all sorts of psychological reasons why he reacts as he does to it. He may have unconscious associations with shapes of this sort, there may even be general tendencies for most normal people to react as he does for which interesting explanations might be forthcoming, but it is in general not true that to react preferentially in this way to such a situation the agent has to be aware of such things. All he need know is that he has such preferences. In the terms of his minimal aim he will seek to preserve any shape to which he reacts favourably over any shape to which he reacts less favourably. Accordingly, he may either in extreme cases seek to erase the mark he has made, or what is more likely, to modify it in some way, most likely by adding a further shape. Only in the unlikely case of his being so delighted by what he has done that he is unable to envisage any alteration that would not make the result less satisfactory to him, will he at this stage let well alone. (We should assume for the purpose of the thought experiment that he does not simply get bored and leave for lunch: part of the question with which we are concerned is what not getting bored amounts to in these sorts of cases.) His next stage is then to make another mark. To this he also may have similar reactions, but now the situation is far more complex, for it may very well be that while each mark on its own may be reacted to in a certain way, together they can be seen as a whole which invites a quite different response. (Two shapes may seem to "kill" one another or to enhance each other.) Except in the case where each has, as it were, a maximal value separately, and the whole also has such a value, the mark-maker is presented with a choice of which features to preserve or to suppress. To make such a choice is to have attended to what has been made in certain interesting ways.

One of these ways has received more philosophical attention than the other. In his paper *On Drawing an Object*[2] Wollheim refers to an exercise which corresponds quite closely to the early stages of this sort of process reporting how "students entering the studio of Hans Hofmann, the father of New York painting, were told as their first assignment to put a black brush-stroke on a white canvas, and then to stand back and observe how the black was on the white." Wollheim points out that it might be equally possible with some black marks on white to observe how the black was behind the white, his point being that what was being invited was a way of seeing, of attending to the shapes, not to the physical fact that as it so happened the black pigment was smeared on top of the white ground. This is clearly right. Even one mark (the first in the series) on a ground makes two shapes at the very least, and one way (certainly an over-simple way) of referring to the alternatives that Wollheim gives is that the students were asked to attend to these two shapes as different shapes. To some extent it is true that to see one shape in this way "on" another is to both distinguish them and at the same time pay more attention to the former than to the latter: not always though—it is, for instance, possible to see an object with a thin base and a more massive top either as top heavy or as bottom-light, what difference there is here is not just a matter of different degrees of attention. For it to be possible that there can be a question of choice presented by a complex of shapes it is obvious enough that one has to be able to pay attention to them as things that can be chosen between.

Paying attention to different aspects of a state of affairs in this way is not quite the same thing as describing it, even when the description is given in some detail. Two people may very well accept the same description of a relatively complex object—as in the case of a pattern of marks on a white ground they may be able to match it against the same photographic reproduction—while attending to its aspects quite differently. In this sense what we might call "aspecting" differs from describing in that an "aspective" disagreement tends to presuppose a descriptive agreement. If one person sees something as black on white, or top-heavy, while another sees it as white on black or as bottom-light, that they can be seeing "it" differently at all presupposes a point of agreement. In the former case this could be brought out by pointing out, as Wollheim in effect does that they are not disagreeing about whether the black pigment happens to be laid on top of the ground, just as they are not concerned with any question of how many inches various points on the edge of the black shape are from the edge of the white, and so on, while in the latter case by observing that "literally speaking" for something to be top-heavy just is for it to be bottom-light. What distinguishes "aspecting" in this sense from describing is very much a question of what sort of speaking "literally speaking" is. This is a quite central philosophical question that I have not space to pursue here.

(It should perhaps be stressed by the way at this point that there seems to be no good reason for regarding seeing something as black on white, or top-heavy as opposed to some other way is a case of seeing it as a representation of something or other. The English phrase "seeing as" covers a multitude of different situations of attending: there seems no warrant on this account to suppose that to see a pattern of black on white, or to see the present situation in a certain country as a threat to world peace, or to see a painting as a portrait of Henry VIII is to thereby do similar things, or to make similar sorts of judgements. If any common idea runs through such a disparate list it may perhaps be that of imposing a pattern of intelligibility on something or other, and that is an idea so wide that it would seem to embrace any distinctions that may be worth making.)[3]

Philosophers, particularly those concerned with aesthetics, have paid some attention to this sort of pattern-aspecting: it would be hardly possible for them to fail to do so in one way or another. But there is another sort of attention that the mark-maker is engaged in that needs stressing also. As the process continues and the designer pays attention to the shapes he produces, their demands on his attention present themselves in terms of his choices and preferences between them: his preferences for later moves in the "game" become progressively constrained by decisions to retain and to modify what he has already done. Since he may find that, however attractive a later shape may be, he cannot include it in the whole, while at the same time preserving what he has previously preferred, the elaboration of the complex he is making will come to involve increasing restrictions on his range of choice. We might imagine such restrictions becoming such that there is no more that can be done that will not tend to conflict with what he has already decided to preserve and develop. In this very schematic way we might say that his design becomes complete when there is no further room for manoeuvre.

Very schematically, we may say that what is being built up is a pattern of decisions of increasing complexity concerning what to keep and what to change. If a standard means-end rationale is linear, this pattern is more that of a tree. The argument, "wanting (seeking, needing) X and knowing Y to be a means to X, other things being equal, do Y" aims at X in the sense that the agent can be sure of wanting X without being sure how to achieve it. By contrast the pattern of thought in this kind of situation modifies his preferences for what he is next to do in terms of what he has preferred to do at an earlier stage. His series of choices could be mapped thus,

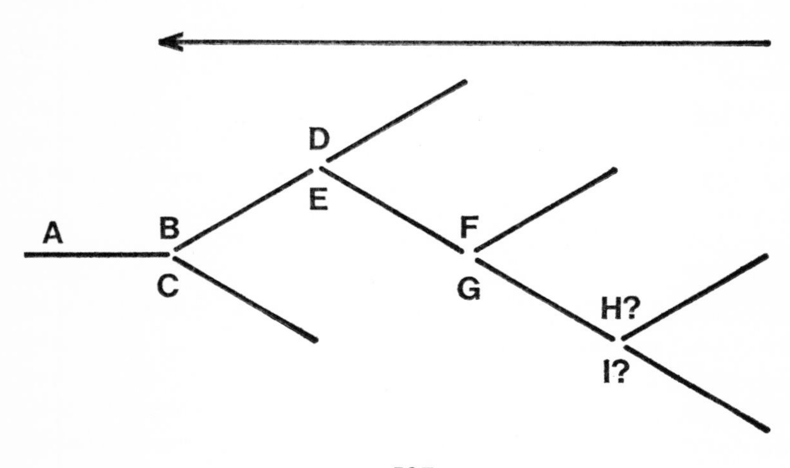

He has reached the position in which the choice between H and I is the option it is in terms of the earlier choices he has made, between A and B and so on. How these choices are presented to him (what makes them intelligible as the choices they are) depends on his knowledge of whence he has come, not on where he intends to go. The marks H and I might even have come about by accident so that his only option is to retain or to erase them. He may not have the least idea what next may be presented to him, yet he can still proceed forward according to an intelligible and developing rationale of action. To do so his understanding has to be directed back to what he has already done.

By contrast, a pattern of decision that is more precisely goal seeking—where the goals are not minimal goals—is forward looking. We can perhaps see the difference most easily if we contrast the case where an agent abandons a "free design" with one where he abandons a means-end project. In the former case he abandons the attempt to preserve even if with modifications, what he has already done or made. In the latter what he abandons is the attempt to achieve what he has not yet done. To discard a design, in the former sense, on which one is working is standardly to throw away or set on one side something that exists already—often a piece of paper, or canvas and paint, some made up material. To abandon a project in the sense of abandoning a goal is not, necessarily not, to discard what already is, but to give up the attempt to make it so. Accordingly, we might map the pattern in these latter cases as,

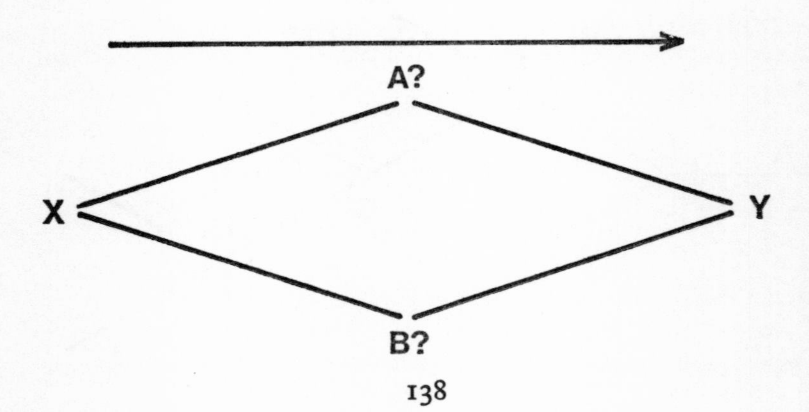

where X represents the situation that the agent sees himself to start from, Y where he wishes to be, or what he wishes to achieve, and the options A and B are concerned with his thought about how to reach Y "from" X. The arrows in the diagrams in each case represent the direction of the agent's attention, what he pays attention to in making his choice. What one pays attention to in choosing provides an answer to the question why one chooses as one does. It is these answers that are articulated as "reasons" where an agent stands aside from his course of action and comments on it, or where it is commented on by others. A further difference between the two models is then that the arrow in the former case points, as it were, to what already is, while in the latter to what is (at best) yet to be.

Similarly contrasting diagrams can be constructed for patterns of explanation of events. On the former model, an event that has just occurred can be explained in terms of those events that have led up to it, even though prediction of the future may be obscure or difficult, while the means-end model compares closely with those patterns of explanation that are also predictive of what in terms of the explanation must be.

Such models are, however, over schematic, not merely in the quite acceptable sense that they are highly simplified but in the sense that they leave important aspects of the situation out of account. In the case of designing one aspect of the story that is left out of account has to do with what it is to pay attention to features of a design. For in practice the two sorts of attention that the designer exercises are closely related to one another.

How closely related they are can be seen if we place the two diagrams together, for what they then suggest is that one may "close" the "tree" at any point and produce a means-end "lozenge",

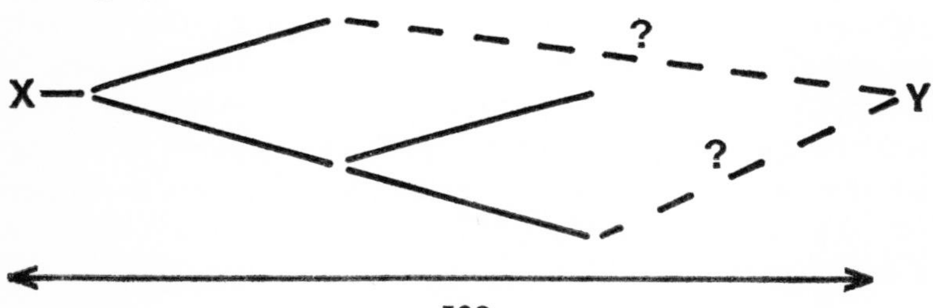

where the agent's attention is directed *both* to what went before as well as to what he can envisage. The diagram permits closure at a whole range of scales in that the agent can envisage some fairly near at hand possible outcome of choice or something further on in his possible activity. A "closed" tree would approximate in words to an agent's question to himself "what shall I do to produce Y?" that is posed in the context of his attention to how he brought himself to the point of making such a choice. While such a judgement may seem complex enough it is perhaps the commonest form of reflection one may engage in in the development of a process of intelligent activity. What the relation of the two diagrams to each other also shows, however, is the degree to which the "tree" represents the most primitive system of practical intelligence in the sense that it underlies any more sophisticated thought in action.

Designers in the course of their designing—and others in more everyday contexts—may pay attention to the features of a complex as features of a design. What is involved in this is such a general matter that it does not seem that one can say very much more about it except that to do so is to regard such features as hanging together in a certain way. In particular cases one may be more specific and it would seem that only then may one say anything of any interest. But the designer—the maker of a pattern—in the process of his making does, in so paying attention, perform a complex sort of mental acts that are interesting in their own right. In the case of a pattern of shapes, colour and texture that he is developing, to regard what he has already made as presenting or constraining options is to attend to it in a quite particular sort of way. To see one colour as "killing" or enhancing another, or a particular shape or texture as contributing to how another shape or texture is seen, is for him to pay attention both to some existing artefact that he has made, but also to it as it was and may be the object of his own attitudes and decisions. In so far as this attention to his past and to its products comes to shape for him the constraints on his further choices, in making them he may "come to know" what he had earlier been concerned with. The process of continuing is also a process of a certain sort of self-discovery.

It is a characteristic of many sorts of activities, by no means confined to the arts, that at a certain point in an agent's endeavours he may find himself saying something like "That's what I now see I have been all along concerned with!" with the force of having made a discovery. Put to the test of a choice one may find that it is constrained by concerns that one had hitherto been unaware of: it is as if the choice itself illuminates its own constraints. Many human relationships are something like this, so also can be certain episodes in the history of the development of certain theories or even political convictions. Anthony Palmer introduced[4] the example of Martin Luther's conviction that the doctrine of salvation by faith alone was in some quite important sense crucial to how he saw himself as a theological rebel into much this sort of context: for the sake of the example it is not important whether or not he in fact said of that insistence that he could "do no other", what is important is that it makes a psychological sense to suppose that he could have. One way of expressing such a sense is that the crucial doctrine at the later time of a crisis of choice became seen as obviously implicit in all that had gone before. It is said of Rubens in painting a certain picture that at a certain point he painted out a whole figure to give a pearl its full lustre; the choice might have gone the other way, that it did not might well have been expressed in the realisation that the interests that constrained the choice were somehow already implicit in the designing that had gone before. To choose otherwise would be somehow to abandon the design. We sometimes say of certain choices that to choose otherwise would "make nonsense of" what has gone before, that not to take a certain stand, not to take a certain course of action would be to break faith with a pattern of past actions.

It is easy to either dismiss this sort of talk as either poetic, mystical, vague in all the bad senses, or else as elliptical either for an appeal to fundamental principles or to over-riding goals. One reason for its seeming to be a mystical thing to say is that if we are to take such declarations seriously we will have to take them to be autobiographical claims in the past tense which are at the same time not memory claims. The agent is not remembering something in saying that he sees that he had been concerned in such a way all along. But he is not straightforwardly inferring it from evidence either. To construe the matter as an appeal to principles is either to say very little, to say little more in effect than that something of general importance for choice is being adverted to, or else to say something false, for in any standard sense of principle-following to follow a principle is to have some standard with which it may be that something yet to be done can be supposed to conform or not conform. Here the point is, that if such principles are implicit, they can only be seen so retrospectively. Very much the same sort of thing goes for goals also. But in fact the simple free-design model can help to illuminate what is going on here, for it provides a picture of how a past course of action can be seen by the agent of it in such a way that it progressively defines his interests. To have made something with conscious and deliberate attention to the options involved in its making is to have made something that one may wish or not to wish to preserve, whether it is a picture of a social state of affairs. Looking back over a relationship, habits that one has developed, that are both the consequences of, and productive of, a pattern of choices and decisions, it may be all *that* one may wish to preserve —that is what has been *made*. Human relationships, such as marriages, love affairs, relationships with children are not *projects* in the sense of being courses of action directed to certain goals. It requires a certain sort of corruption of mind to see them as goal-directed activities and to engage in them thus. A way of putting this can be to say that they are "processes of making".

Not all the constraints on further action that may be built up as the pattern of activity, and of what is made, progresses need be those mental constraints that have to do with conserving preferences. In some cases they may be mechanical, though in ways that are not without some interest. Perhaps the simplest case of all would be one where a tool, such as a chisel, may together with the wood already cut, act as its own jig, the part of the tool that is behind the cutting edge by resting on the previously cut surface guiding its own cut. The skill of using such tools, which are often rather naturally associated with a certain sort of hand-made artefact, has often held a peculiar fascination as a metaphor for an important kind of mental discipline. This need not be altogether surprising, for the skill involved in "letting the tool do the job" can be a peculiarly subtle one involving as it does a continuous interplay of attention between the regularities imposed by what one has already done and what one has it in mind to do. To look back having put one's hand to the plough is not only to miss sight of where one intends to go, but also what is surely the real point of the idiom, to fail to concentrate on how the plough itself is able to guide its own cut.

If we examine a more complex activity of this sort in any detail we may come to see how the skeletal model of quite free design may be modified to take account of those activities that are constrained by a search for goals or by obedience to recipes. Someone (say) carving leaves in wood (an example that notoriously, and significantly, obsessed such people as William Morris) needs to pay attention to three quite different sorts of things at the same time. Certain patterns of shapes, rhythmic curves for instance, may, as in the case of a quite free design, be developed preserved or modified as the maker builds up his pattern of decisions about them. At the same time they are the curves of natural objects to which he needs to pay attention. To the extent that he does, that he wishes to copy such natural shapes he will be modifying what he does in terms of a certain goal (often quite precisely defined by a working drawing). As well as this the ways in which his tools will naturally run will be constrained not only by the physical cuts that have been made before, but by the materials that he is using, by the grain of the wood, and so on. Part of the satisfaction of looking at a carved object of this sort can derive from our ability to see in the completed artefact a testimony to these ways in which the maker's activity has been constrained by this sort of attention. We may thus infer something concerning what has been attended to. The object makes sense to us as made in this way. To so respond to such an object is to see the evidence of, among other things, a process of thought.

In his book *The Nature of Art and Workmanship*,[5] David Pye rightly points out that the somewhat obsessive belief of such people as Ruskin and Morris in the pre-eminent value of what is hand-made, in this way can be both sentimental and confused. It is certainly not the case that things made in other sorts of ways need lack qualities of beauty and interest that can be present in hand-made objects, nor is it true that only such work is or ought to be a source of legitimate pleasure to a maker of something. As Pye and many others have pointed out, something designed while it is made need neither be a superior object in itself to any other, nor need the activity of designing while making be a superior activity. My concern is simply with the philosophical interest of such cases, with the sense in which the objects themselves may be able to show us something, and with what that sort of thing is. Nonetheless, such activities do have a definite philosophical importance.

If a process of thought is revealed by "action painting" it is simpler. It too may be typically revealed in the completed artefact. It is significant that a painter such as Jackson Pollock characteristically used paint of different textures and miscibilities in such a way that it is relatively easy to see that one layer, or dribble of paint lies (literally) on top of or underneath another. This can make it possible to see the finished product to some extent—not by any means completely—as having been made in a certain temporal sequence. Of course nobody looking at such a painting will be inclined to calculate the sequence very precisely, but it shows itself in the way in which it may seem that the textures and patterns are "built up". (To a considerable extent this quality can be present in all oil painting. As we have already seen, this is one of the main factors that tells against a practical possibility of fully reproducing such things, for such qualities are in most such cases important to how we respond to the completed objects.) This sense of the thing's having been built up can be seen as corresponding to the thought process of building up a design. It is sometimes said that such paintings "represent" the very action of the painter in painting them. We need to have some care concerning the sense of "represent" here, however. (In his paper *On Drawing an Object*[6] Wollheim suggests that there is no reason why we should not take it that to see a shape as lying in front of another, but not in that literal sense that means that it is physically placed on top of it is to see it representationally. Both ways of seeing something "on top of another" are involved in seeing a built up texture of patterned paint as indicative of a built up design, for the "literal" way in which this is so will be a consequence of the order of the maker's actions while the sense that is not literal is essential to those judgements and choices that he will have made in designing and thus to see the object as designed in this way is also to see the elements of the design in ways that, while not identical to how he may have seen them, do correspond to how he may well be supposed to have done so, or to be inviting us to. But it would not be quite correct to see the result as a picture of his activity in designing, or a model of it, plan of it, or whatever.) This is not because the concepts of representation here are not very general, and it is certainly not because of any suggestion that for one thing to represent another it is to give an illusion of it, or to closely resemble it. Models, blue-prints and so on are clearly in this sense representational. It is rather, because the connection between the artefact that is an outcome of the activity of making it that is designed while being made in this way, and the activity itself is more intimate than that. The sense in which such things represent the appropriate activities is more like, though not quite identical to, that in which we might say that a vote in the Commons represents a victory for, or a change of heart by, the Government, namely that in which it is evidence for, or even constitutes, these things. The artefact in this case is a testimony to a process of design in that sense in which it can be seen as its visible outcome. As it was completed a process of thought was completed.

To complete such a "free" design is to reach a stage in a pattern of choice and decision in which there is no room for further modification consistent with the preceding choices. To see it thus is, in terms of what one may see as evidence of such choices, not to be able to envisage such modifications. It is partly this that those who have conceived of the judgement of a design as satisfactory have been inclined to identify as the perception of something's having an "organic unity", and it is sometimes supposed that such a concept has to do solely with the arts, or with aesthetic judgement. But this can be misleading.

It can be misleading to suppose this so long as such a supposition carries with it the suggestion either that only works of art can be, or should be, seen in this way, or the suggestion that this is the only fundamentally relevant way of regarding something aesthetically, or that freely designing, as opposed to the pursuit of goals should be understood in terms of such completions. None of these things follow. It may be perfectly relevant to responding to, and coming to understand all sorts of works of art that we should see them as having, or not having, achieved certain ends, goals or intentions. Not all cases of designing as one makes are cases of designing works of art, just as very few works of art are simply of that sort, and there may be many activities of this sort that cannot be completed, yet may still be found intelligible in these terms. What is exemplified by a "free design" is something quite general.

What, then, does the "experiment" of a "free design" show us? Perhaps the first thing that we should note is that being able to be recognised as finished or completed is not essential to such a process of thought in action. An abstract design on a finite area of canvas is, for example, to be so completed very largely because the field of possible action is materially limited by among other things the edges of the surface to be coloured. Other such material limits may be involved, in other cases for example, limits of time. But a pattern of choices that builds itself up as it goes along need not be end-stopped in this way. Courses of activity that may extend over many years, or even be engaged in by more than one person may also be regarded in this way. The progress of Mondrian's painting from his early representational drawing of a tree to his later abstracts might very reasonably be regarded as such a continuing process of the building up of constraints on choices, of exploring the "implications" of what had gone before. To so regard a process of activity need not be to see it as either directed to, nor as leading to, its own completion. Any "creative" writer, even a philosopher, may in this way go on from where he was, step by step, without necessarily either looking for a completion of what he is doing, not even it making very much sense to suppose what such a thing would be. To see an activity of this sort as an intelligible process is to regard it retrospectively, and such a view need have no implications concerning a possible completion.

Perhaps the simplest highly general example of this sort may be provided by the history of scientific enquiry. Such a history is perhaps above all else a way of seeing that any such stage in the activity is one that depended on, was constrained by, interests decisions, ways of thinking and describing that preceded it. To see the history of a process of thought (in this case that of a community rather than an individual) is to see any later stage as an intelligible development from an earlier one. It would be a rather obvious fallacy to conclude from this either that the earlier stages in such a process were such that the later stages could have been predicted from them or that the process should be interpreted as leading to some final stage of completion. The history of any such process of thought is well able to say that the process is progressive in the sense that any later stage may, with more or less precision, be related to some earlier one in the sense that it may be shown even to have been impossible except in relation to it without in the least being able to say that such a progression points to a final conclusion. In this sense, for example, Newton "stood on the shoulders of giants", but any view of "scientific progress" in a sense that looks forward to some completed future state must go beyond whatever evidence that may make the history of such thought intelligible. The temptation towards such a fallacious conclusion is at least partly responsible for the feeling that a retrospective historical account of human activity that makes it an intelligible process of thought and decision (in some very general manner) somehow "ought" to be able to make corresponding predictions (in some equally general manner). But in such an area it may be a simple fact both that we can only understand retrospectively, and that the agents of the process may only be able to conceive their constraints in this way. In the spirit of our thought-experiment, the canvas of real life has no frame around it.

Of course such general patterns of activity do involve goals and principles: it is only in the case of highly generalised accounts of the processes as a whole that these can be disregarded. Does our thought-experiment throw any light on the relation of these to such general patterns of activity?

The picture that emerges would seem to be something like this.

A goal, in the sense that an activity may be directed towards it, is a situation imagined or envisaged by the agent. A condition of being able to direct an activity towards some goal is thus to be able to imagine or envisage something with more or less precision. It is this, somewhat trivial fact, that indicates what there is in common between the completion of a free design and the successful completion of any other course of activity, the difference being simply that in the case of goal directed activity what one envisaged is recognised as having been realised, while in the former case the negative condition holds of not being able to envisage anything further that will enhance, rather than conflict with what went before. In each case what is involved is an imagined state of affairs to which the agent has a preference. As we have seen in the case of the simplest means-end activities and the arguments that justify them, even to choose X as a means to Y is to make a choice among a range of imagined states of affairs. Practical thought is essentially a matter of choosing what is either in fact before one or can be imagined to be. It is equally trivial that an imagined state of affairs may thus do duty for, or stand in for, an actual one. We would be hard put to it in most practical situations were this not so. In the simplified case of someone constructing a design as he goes along, it would be a strangely ignorant designer who could not ever imagine how various further steps in his progress might go, could not extend the process in his head to some degree. How far his ability to imagine how another shape or colour might modify what he has already done can be relied on will depend on such things as his experience of colours and shapes, his general knowledge of their compatibilities and incompatibilities and so on. The more he can imagine ahead of the game in this way the nearer to a goal directed activity what he is doing will become: he can try for a certain result since he can envisage how such a result will be. Similarly, his past experience of how such shapes and colours have tended to fit together in other situations can provide him with practical principles, recipes, for how to achieve such effects. His ability to formulate goals and principles of practical action of the sort that may be of any help to him in his exercise will depend on the degree of his practical experience in the field. Conversely, what he imagines will always be open to falsification by experience; colours and shapes may not turn out just as he imagines them, and as he imagines further steps beyond the immediate situation so this chance will be likely to increase. He will have to explore the possibilities practically. His past, learnt, practical knowledge can only take him so far.

It may be felt that this is especially the case in aesthetic contexts, that what we are faced with in this sort of case is just another example of the general principle that within that context the role of general principles and practical recipes is limited, more limited than in more "mundane" areas. But if this is so it is only so to the extent that one of the many things that the arts is concerned with is to explore the possibilities of the limits of what can be imagined or envisaged beyond experience. There is no reason to suppose that the general principles of the nature of thought in action are any different. However far one may be able to rely on one's past experience of those possible situations to which one may have a preference, or on the experience of others who have reported on similar situations, even in moral contexts (where one may have to choose and act on preferences concerning the situations of people) one may still have to be prepared to test one's learnt principles and imagined goals against one's actual responses to actual situations. The *generality* of morals depends on the important fact that in many cases one may imagine very well how one will react, what choices one will make. The equally important *particularity* of moral responsibility, that requires one to pay attention to what one is doing, that requires the exercise of thought in action as well as about action, depends on the fact that one cannot always do so. The possibility of acting on principle does not absolve one from the responsibility to react, to make decisions and choices in actual, as opposed to envisaged, situations. General practical principles to have any value, envisaged goals, envisaged in terms of responsible judgement (in other words the agent's actual choices and preferences for which he can take responsibility) are possible if it is possible to imagine states of affairs to which one may respond, and that is possible only so long as one is prepared to respond to actual states of affairs.

I have here deliberately restricted my account of "retrospective understanding" in an activity to those cases where the agent is an individual, whether he is a painter, a writer of a philosophy essay or even someone making a flower arrangement. We need to begin with simple cases. What I have not considered, and to do so in any detail would take me well beyond the scope of the present study, is how such an account might be extended to group activity, group composition or more generally, and ultimately more importantly what might be called social creativity which includes, of course, such activities as political movements. At this point it would be absurd to explore such matters in any very realistic detail, but it should not be impossible to indicate what sorts of complications such an investigation would be likely to encounter and what the main shape of the picture would be.

Somewhat over-schematically, we could make a start by considering two people developing a pattern of activity together. We might even consider the development of a friendship, or a love affair. It is illuminating that some of our commonest idioms in this area have to do with making, not merely that we say that they make friends or make love, but more significantly, that they may refer to what they are engaged in in terms of making—their characteristic loyalties to which they appeal in deciding how to act further together are to what they have "made" together, to something that has been built up. It is equally significant that it is almost wholly absurd to refer to such activities as "projects", for what constrains their choices, the pattern of preferences that they put before one another, is a progressive attention to what they have done, to what they may value, or fail to value in that. Of course they may develop goals and ambitions, but it is a feature of their thought in what they do being internal to their relationship, rather than being externally imposed by duties and obligations to others or by prior principles of right behaviour, that such goals as they do envisage will emerge from the context of their continuing relationship. A more or less infallible method for disrupting such a "creative" partnership can be to ask what its aims are and this is not because to do so is to break some pattern of mutual self deception (though this is always possible) but because such a question is shatteringly irrelevant to their pattern of activity.

In a not quite dissimilar manner a design team may spend a large part of its internal discussion in forms of debate and social activity that are effectively concerned with ways of attending to the emerging pattern of its own activities, with attempting to find out what it is that it is really concerned with. If we think in terms of projects and goals as something that may be set to the team externally this sort of activity can easily seem to be a mere waste of time, maybe pleasant, perhaps psychologically or socially useful, but in principle a non-rational diversion from the main task of getting things done in the most efficient way. But again, while such a team will certainly have its goals, and have been set them, such goals must of necessity, so long as the object of the exercise is to exploit the creativity and invention of the team, not be enough. A sense of what they are doing has to emerge in just the same way as an individual agent has to pay attention to what he is doing—future action, further choices and preferences, can here too only emerge from the constraints of attention to what has been done.

Such co-operative activities may of course fail, and when they do the significant factor in their failure can be, not a confusion of aims among those involved but a failure to understand and attend fully to each other's attitudes (loyalties or rejections) to what has gone before. It should not therefore surprise us that urgent pressure from outside the group to define a clear common aim may actually be disruptive, for it will be in those cases where what they are being told is what they already know. What they may not know (may not for all sorts of reasons such as mutual dislike or misunderstanding be able to attend to) is how they reached the point in their activities which has become a dead end. Creativity may sometimes require that one does look back having put one's hand to the plough—or, to put the matter another way, the activity may just not be like ploughing.

If we turn to even larger scale corporate activities these speculations can present a not unfamiliar picture. Central, for instance, to a Marxist view of society and of political action within it is the idea that a sense of history is integral with our ability as free political agents to exercise our thought in the action of changing society. In the most general terms the promise is that the manner of making our world over anew takes its stand not, or not primarily, on some envisaged goal or Utopian blue-print for an ideal post-revolutionary state to be worked towards but on a form of understanding of the processes of the past that is itself part and parcel of intelligent present social and political activity. Marxist scholars as well as their opponents may see this as a ludicrous oversimplification, but it is still largely true that it is in terms of something like this oversimplification that much of the standard philosophical attacks on Marxism can be seen, for the questions that seem most naturally to arise is whether we are to take the main lines of the doctrine as requiring us to suppose that history determines the future—in which case the revolution is inevitable whatever anyone may do about the matter—or as a voluntaristic doctrine, in which case what of the "objective facts of history", which no choosing can alter? And finally, it is urged, what sort of a society are the revolutionaries really aiming at, can they even imagine it, and if not how can they know the end is worth the means to it? However, if we do make a simple generalisation of the thought-experiment of designing while making into these larger political contexts it will be something like these simple, if apparently objectionable, doctrines that will follow quite directly.

They will follow because if we are to extend a picture of creative thought in action to include thought in political and social action, that too will be a matter of the agents' understanding of what they want, and thus their ability to envisage their own goals, as opposed to externally imposed goals, emerging in their retrospective attention to their past patterns of activity. In the largest scale of all this will mean the history of that society, of its institutions and ideas, of which their activity is a part. Long before Marx, Vico referred to this sort of understanding in social and political action as "makers' knowledge", not because someone, or some group, who have made something have necessarily better knowledge of its working principles or a privileged access to how it might be made, but because this sort of knowledge is part of their thought *in* what they do—their knowledge of how the social developments of which they were a part itself develops with their thought in action. A Marxist picture of thought in political action in effect implies that authentic activity that unites political thought and intelligence with its expression in practice stands threatened by two opposite temptations. On the one hand there is the temptation of "Utopianism" which involves the normally self-deluded belief that one does know just what it is that one is aiming for, what one wants, what the ideal final political state should be. This is normally self deluding partly because it is not normally given to anyone to envisage anything of that nature clearly or distinctly enough, and partly because, while someone or some group may be told what they should seek and accept that they should do so, such acceptance is unlikely to correspond to anything that might emerge from their own attention to their experience and decision—as if we might manage to tell two friends what the aims of their friendship should be. On the other hand, such authentic action can be threatened by the temptation of that sort of nihilism that compares very closely with the position of one who working on his design comes to the conclusion, not merely that it is *hard* to see what can be made of what he has done, difficult to see how it might be developed, but impossible. (As where the painting is neither finished nor unfinished but has reached a dead end.) A painter who tears up what he is doing and starts again has to that extent abandoned his creative activity. This may be justified where all that is at risk is a piece of canvas and a few hour's work. It is much less justifiable if what is at risk is a pattern of human relationships, and perhaps never justifiable if what is at risk is a human society. Creative activity may, of course, be radical and drastic. Rubens' painting out a whole figure to give a pearl its full lustre was, if one likes, a revolution within the activity of painting that picture and painting a picture or writing an essay may be a series of such "revolutions"; if we extend these analogies it may not be too far fetched to see social and political revolutions in this light.

To extend this account in this way can in one sense be little more than speculative. Certainly it can offer no more than a tentative sketch, but what is less speculative (certainly less than that for any serious account of Marx) is that we need not be bound by a picture of intelligence that makes knowing just what one wants and seeking to achieve it the sole test of rationality. It is a form of rationality, in some contexts a vital element of intelligent behaviour, but it is not at the core of the matter.

Put like this, the claim that the sort of thinking that is involved in designing is logically primitive to that practical thinking that is goal directed or governed by principles, expresses very little more than the claim that experience of what is the case is a condition for realistically imagining what might be. But this little more may still be of some importance, for what it argues is that a model of rationality that is based solely on goals and principles is one that is divorced from the roots of thought in action. It is in reacting to what one has done, acting and reacting to the material world, the world in which one may make and design, that one formulates and comes to know what one's goals are, what one is concerned with, and what one's practical principles can be, just as the conception of the object one is making can be developed in the process of making it, and must be in the process of designing it. In this sense the root concept of practical thinking should be thought in the process of making.

It is often supposed that activity that is not goal directed and which does not follow pre-established practical principle for action must be not only unplanned but also unpurposive and thus random and that in so far as it is random it could not show intelligence, could not be an exercise of mind. None of this follows. On the contrary, if anything in what I am arguing is correct, that sort of creative activity that has traditionally presented such a scandal to our very idea of intelligence is nothing more than the exercise of practical thought in its simplest and most elementary form. While it should be a standing disgrace to traditional and orthodox views of intelligence that they are not able to distinguish between such vastly different activities as random doodling and attentive designing, we should conclude, rather, that any theory of intelligence worth its salt should *begin* with a theory of free creativity and that, moreover, it should not be too difficult a task to do this. (In my examples I have not unnaturally considered the natural intelligence of people in their everyday affairs, but there seems to be no reason why these general conclusions should not also apply in principle to any theory of artificial intelligence as well.)[7]

In terms of the foregoing account, however, we are left with a further issue concerning the hierarchy of presuppositions in the model of free designing. This is that which is concerned to the attention which the maker of the design pays to how he sees what he has made, to what I have called his capacity to "aspect" as opposed to describe what is before him. It is somewhere in this area that a connection between the thought that can be involved in making and the maker's understanding of how the world is, needs paying attention to. Accordingly, I shall attempt to round off this account of thinking and making by touching somewhat sketchily on that. Here also we may find the thought-experiments that may take place in the activities of artists illuminating.

Notes

1 As Kant saw very clearly in the *Critique of Judgment*.
2 cf. R. Wollheim, *On Drawing an Object*, Inaugural Lecture, University College London, 1964.
3 Wollheim does, however, really wish to regard such a case as one of representation since it essentially involves seeing a two dimensional object as (another) three dimensional one. In many cases it may be pedantic to quibble over whether it is this or rather a matter of seeing what is two dimensional as if it were three dimensional, which would not, for me, be a matter of representation.
4 *op. cit.*
5 David Pye, *The Nature and Art of Workmanship*, Studio Vista, 1968.
6 *op. cit.*
7 Since composing my own thoughts on creativity I am grateful to Dr. Margaret Boden for directing my attention to Walter R. Reitman's book *Cognition and Thought, An information Processing approach*, J. Wiley & Sons, New York 1965, and especially to his Chapter Six, "Creative Problem Solving; Notes from the Autobiography of a Fugue". This chapter is based on a brief case study of a composer's thought in and about his activity of solving the "problem" of writing a fugue and a great deal of what he has to say relates quite closely to my own account, as does his attempt to

place models derived from these sorts of examples within a general theory of intelligence (in his case a model of artificial intelligence). Unfortunately I came across Reitman's study too late for me to do more than to acknowledge it here.

CHAPTER SIX

MAKING PICTURES

VERY few paintings are free designs of the kind that could even sympathetically be regarded as providing material for the sort of thought-experiment considered in the previous chapter. Most are, of course, pictures of things.[1] Pictures are at one and the same time both made objects and also representations of actual or possible states of affairs. If the experiment of isolating an element of free designing from the complex of activities involved in the visual arts is to have any general value for a practical understanding of the sorts of cummunication that may be involved in that field of human activity, and certainly if such experiments may be said to show anything of more general philosophical interest, we must at the very least be able to show how we might build onto our understanding of this relatively impoverished activity some better understanding of more complex procedures. We may need to ask, among other things, whether the picture of making a free design can show us something about what may be involved in making a representation.

There can be two sorts of reasons why such a question, apart from any intrinsic interest it may have, is pressing at this point. On the one hand, as far as the activities of artists are concerned, to suggest, as I have done, that we may see the stylistic episodes of twentieth-century painting as a (perhaps not very systematic, or very conscious) process of analysis requires that we should be able to see any one such episode as part of such a whole. If such things as action painting are claimed to have an extrinsic interest in terms of a general problem, to make such a claim good requires that we say something concerning other aspects of that problem. On the other hand, paintings, drawings and pictures of various sorts are not the only kinds of artefacts that may incorporate in one way or another their maker's knowledge and beliefs about how the world is or how it may be. Stories, diagrams, descriptions, theories of different kinds, either very down to earth theories or very abstract and formal ones, are, along with mathematical constructions and things of that sort, as much to be numbered among what may be made as chairs, pies and patterns may be. All of these former sorts of artefacts present a particular variety of problem for any account of thought in making. They all in one way or another raise a question about a possible relationship between that practical sort of thought that is involved in making and what would seem to be those less practical sorts of thinking that have to do with judgements, thoughts, discoveries and reports of how things are or may be supposed to be.

Rather clearly, to attempt any general and systematic survey of these wider philosophical topics would be beyond the scope of the present enquiry which is concerned merely to insist on the general relevance of the very idea of the thought that may be involved in making things to our understanding of understanding. It is not my purpose to survey what would, on this view of the matter, amount to the whole, or at all events a very large part of, the field of possible philosophical investigation. It would be silly to attempt such a task. On the other hand, it is hard to see how even the suggestion that the intelligible process of making something could have any philosophical importance at all could have much point to it without at least suggesting how one might proceed further.

What I shall, accordingly, attempt here is first of all a sketch of how the process of making may be seen to extend into just one sort of *belief*-incorporating artefact, namely pictures, and then to suggest, rather more sketchily, how the wider philosophical landscape might look from such a vantage point. Inevitably, such a way of proceeding will be somewhat speculative. My only excuse for that can be that it may sometimes be of value to indicate the sorts of enquiries that others may be better able to proceed with. It is often more the business of philosophers to ask questions than to provide answers to them. Sometimes, too, it may be useful to ask for questions.

Before doing so, it may be convenient to summarise the position so far. What has been contended in general is first of all that while much of our practical thinking can be understood in terms of an agent's following certain practical principles, or of his seeking to accomplish certain goals, not all intelligible practical activity can be, or should be, viewed in this way, and that even when we can reasonably view it thus how an agent understands those practical principles that he is following, or conceives of the end he is seeking, cannot be divorced from his experience with the materials of his actions.

A condition of our being able to understand the activities of those who do things and make things with the world around them is that we should distinguish between two sorts of account of what might be called an agent's rationale. On the one hand we may refer to a set of practical propositions which he may accept concerning what ought to be done under certain circumstances, or what should be done if certain sorts of situations or states of affairs are to be brought about. Such propositions are typically the sorts of statements that occur in manuals or textbooks or in moral or legal codes of conduct, or which may be expressed by one person to another in teaching, or advising, ordering, commending or justifying what someone has done or may do. They are what an instructor may impart to an apprentice, or what an administrator or legislator may express or debate. It is in expressing such practical propositions that a person may most properly be said to be concerned with "reasons for action". A conception of rationality that construes rationality in terms of reasons effectively restricts the scope of claiming or denying that someone is rational or irrational to those contexts where such reasons for acting may be involved. To concentrate an account of practical thinking on this area alone is, in effect, to present a picture of the intelligibility of someone's actions that places the thought of advisors, teachers and administrators at the centre of the stage of rationality, while at the same time making the thought of those whose reflection and concentration issues most naturally in what they do, as opposed to what they say, correspondingly less intelligible. It has the further consequence of making that sort of activity that is sometimes called "creative" essentially non-rational in that it cannot be construed in terms of following reasons for action.

The other sort of account we may give of that kind of thought that may be involved in practice has to do with what we might call his thought *in* what he does as opposed to his thought about or concerning what he does. This need not be expressed by the agent in the form of statements concerning what ought to be done or why things ought to be done, indeed he may not be able to express such claims in such cases, as with many acts of speech, his thought can only be understood as directly expressed in action. To investigate such thought we need to pay attention to the structure of his attention to what it is that he is doing and to the circumstances of his doing it. In the sort of practical contexts in which this applies how he attends cannot be identified independently from the pattern of his choices, preferences and decisions.

The claim that so-called "free design" represents practical thinking at its most primitive then amounts to this. What such activity, at least in terms of the somewhat idealised model we have considered, is free of is the agent's attending to what lies outside that structure of choices and attention which has as its outcome what he has made or constructed. The simplest model of thought in action in this sense then has the agent paying retrospective attention to what he has already done as he decides on what he should do further. Constraints on his further choices then derive simply from what he may come to see as consistent or inconsistent with how he has already acted. There may be general principles of consistency of various sorts involved in this, but it may also be central to the nature of the agent's thought in such an activity that he will not be able to formulate them until very much later in the process, when he is able to pay attention to his own process of making as he can look back over it. By contrast, to act in accordance with principles for action that can be expressed by the agent to himself in advance of his own activity, or to seek ends or goals that may be formulated with any degree of precision in advance, is to attend to intellectual constraints on choice that have an origin in his thought outside the confines of that particular pattern of action. To seek a goal, or to follow a recipe for achieving an intended goal, is to that extent to go beyond that form of thought that follows an activity, as an argument may be followed, "whithersoever it leads". To follow either an argument, or a process of action, whithersoever it leads is certainly for choices, decisions and preferences, and the actions that accord with them, to be constrained and guided by thought, but it is not to be constrained by what may be formulated independently, or in advance of, those actions with which they have to do.

Since to remember how we have acted before and learn from our experience, or learn from the experience of others, envisage and imagine desirable possible outcomes for our actions, or the actions of others, is essential to even the most minimally reflective and intelligent rational agent, it would clearly be silly to suppose either that quite pure cases of "free" design and invention need be very common in practice or that patterns of activity of that sort would themselves be capable of providing all the requirements of intelligent behaviour. In much the same way it might be said that to attempt to rely exclusively on our own immediate experience of things would hardly get us very far in this world. But it would be equally mistaken to conclude thereby that such "primitive" forms of activity are not forms of thought in action. On the contrary, if we are to make sense of the very idea of the processes of growth of practical knowledge and experience, we must regard them as of quite central importance. The very idea of designing *in* making, *as* making proceeds, is essential to that of our understanding being able to grow and develop.

In view of the fact that we rightly tend to associate such notions as creativity and inventiveness with imaginativeness, however, such a conclusion may seem to have an air of paradox. For the idea of imaginativeness surely suggests, among other things, the idea of someone's being able to imagine, or to envisage, something other than what is, or what can be attended to in what is. The picture of purely retrospective constraints of attention in a free design to what has already been done seems to rule this out. Is this not to exclude from such a picture of "creative" activity its most important feature? A way of responding to this may be, however, to point to a distinction that arises directly from the concept of a free design itself. There are two ways in which we might think of someone's coming to envisage a particular outcome for such an activity and so enriching the constraints on his choices by working towards it. On the one hand, we might suppose his being asked or instructed by someone else, as a designer might be by a client, to work to such an end, or he might derive an idea of what he wishes to aim towards from some tradition that he accepts that assumes certain outcomes as acceptable and others as not. On the other hand, we might suppose him to envisage and desire a possible outcome of what he is doing and work towards it as a consequence of having imagined for himself how, among various alternatives, what he is doing might work out. In this latter case he is, as it were, working out "in his head" as opposed to in practice, possible developments of his own activity. Such working out may be careful and meticulous, or it may be closer to intuitive guess-work, but either way it is still a working out of that process of activity which is his and not another's: more importantly, what he envisages, though a goal, an end state of affairs, is imagined as an end state of a process. It is attended to, or conceived as, the limit of an imagined procedure, not as some possible state of affairs that may be considered quite independently of some way of supposing how he, the agent, may reach it. To be sure, one may easily enough imagine and desire some state of affairs without in the least being able to conceive how one may achieve it, and such wishes may show great originality in the sense that few others may have thought of such things as desirable, or indeed thought of them at all, but this can be distinguished from that sort of inventiveness that envisages something as a new possibility, and it is that which derives from the agent's own awareness of his own processes of action or imagined action.

To say this is, however, to need to make a further distinction. For if some part of what I am arguing is not to collapse, it will be necessary to distinguish between what I have called envisaging something as the outcome of a possible course of action or design —for example a process of making—and merely envisaging something as an end to be sought and then being able to imagine how it might be achieved. In the former case, but not in the latter, there must be some sense to the suggestion that *how* the outcome is envisaged is in an important sense part and parcel of how it is envisaged as the outcome of a process of achieving it. For any "willed end" it may be that to will an end is to will a means to it—at all events in that sense in which the responsibility for so willing requires that he who wills it must also be responsible for the means he chooses to adopt—but the account of creativity and invention we are here concerned with requires more than that in these former cases, that somehow the very idea of what is to be sought should be conceived of in terms of the relevant process of activity. Perhaps the best chance of showing what may be involved in these cases is to return to further examples of a maker's activity. So let us return to the question of picture-making.

We might begin by asking what further constraints on his choices and decisions the maker of a picture of something has beyond those which can apply to the maker of a free abstract design. The most obvious answer must be that as well as attending to what he is making he must attend to the object he is attempting to depict or to how he supposes some imagined, or possible object should be. The artefact that he is constructing needs to be compared with a real or an imagined object. In his account of the activity of a painter in painting a picture, Gombrich in his book *Art and Illusion*[2] described him as "making and matching", and at first sight the suggestion that this is what is involved seems obvious enough. We may imagine the maker of a painting or a drawing before some object that he wishes to depict and making some shape, either as the more or less random first mark in a sketch, or with the intention of its resembling some seen part or aspect of the object, and then comparing the two. In terms of how he compares the two things he sees, he may then modify the mark that he has made to bring the likeness closer. We may thus imagine his process of making a picture of the object as a step by step process of production and adjustment with the general intention of producing an artefact that may as nearly as possible visually resemble the visible object that is to be depicted. But, even if a true account of what the painter does to describe his activity this can give rise to a variety of questions and difficulties. Perhaps the most obvious of these difficulties has to do with what happens in those cases where he is painting or drawing, not some object that is directly before him but something that he merely imagines, when he does not paint from life.

We could, of course, say that he matches what he makes with how he imagines that object to be, but at best this would be to say little more than that he is painting something that he imagines and does not see, and is at worst profoundly obscure. For what sort of activity of imagination and perception is it that is involved in comparing what is seen with what is imagined as visible? Certainly, one may ask oneself of a drawing of something remembered whether "that" is indeed "how it looked", but it is by no means clear that such a question supposes some resemblance between something made and something imagined. One may, for example, be fairly sure that a drawing that one has made does not visually resemble an object that one remembers, even though one may be unable to recall quite how it was that the object did look: one is simply confident enough that at all events it did not look quite like that. Sometimes indeed, one may suppose someone making a drawing and concluding at a certain point "Ah yes, that is how it looked." The recognition that the drawing was successful is part and parcel of the successful recollection of the object. Up to that point it is by no means clear what would count at all as a progressive matching and adjustment of one thing to another, even if we allow that there need be no difficulty concerning the comparison of something seen with the recollection of something. The case is still more difficult with the idea of matching something made to something wholly imaginary. Certainly, it is possible enough to suppose someone able to vividly and clearly visualise an imagined object and proceeding to produce some actual seen thing that looked the same, but drawing imaginary objects does not have to be like that. When a child is encouraged by his teacher to draw an imaginary dragon, he is not asked to match anything with anything else, but to imagine something as he draws it—"Let's make him green, and shall we give him great big teeth like that, and then will those blue bits be his eyes on the top of his head . . .?" A picture of an imaginary dragon neither resembles, nor fails to resemble, either an imaginary object or the visual image of such an object. It is a picture of a dragon that was thought up, invented, imagined as the picture was thought up, invented and made. A picture of a dragon is just as much a picture of a dragon whether or not dragons are real or imaginary. It indeed looks like a dragon, but we should not conclude from that that there is some dragon that looks like it.

It can be all too easy to be misled by the fact that we may quite properly say of certain pictures that they look like certain things, real or imaginary, that therefore those things look like them. Normally, if A looks like B, or simply resembles B, B looks like or resembles A, but we should be on our guard against supposing a similar symmetry in these cases. But, surely, it may be felt, there could hardly be any point in saying anything like "Tommy's picture looks like a green dragon" unless there were some pressure towards such a symmetry in the general context of the idiom, even though it should be resisted in the case of certain specific claims that employ it. If Tommy's photograph looks like him, doesn't he then to that extent look like his photograph? Perhaps all we mean by saying that his picture looks like a dragon is that if there were such a dragon then we can be sure it would look like that?

In many ways drawing dragons raises just the same difficulties, open to much the same answers, as describing dragons does. A child's description of a dragon in a story no more matches a dragon than his drawing does, since there is no such animal for it to match, yet it is a description of a dragon, in a story about dragons, for all that. The story contains a description of how a dragon might be, or at all events for the child who makes the story up, how he imagines or supposes how it might be. When a child, or any other author, makes up a story about a dragon, or any other fictional creature, his making up the story is not a different activity from his making up the fictional creatures, and other things and events which the story is about. Similarly, to get a child to follow a story that he is being told is to get him to suppose, or imagine what the story is concerned with.

Perhaps the simplest way of construing the "logical structure" of fictions is to see them as being very similar indeed, if not identical to, suppositions. The expression "once upon a time", which children often require stories to be introduced by as a way of indicating that what they are about to hear is fiction and not fact, has much the same force as the expression "suppose". A story may in this way fail to make sense, fail to hang together, or be "true to life", in much the same way as a supposition may. We might imagine someone making up a story with a child; "If (we suppose that) the dragon had great big teeth, do you think he'd bite people with them?" "No, he was a nice dragon. His teeth were for eating great big flowers." That is *one* way of making his great big teeth consistent with his being a nice dragon. The passage of thought involved in such a childish case is only simpler, but not different in its essential form from that involved in, for example, criticising a novel for not being true to life, or praising it for the contrary virtue. Given that the hero was such and such, and inhabited a world that was as described, would he have behaved as the story asks us to suppose he did? Certain elements in a story are in other words, what we are to suppose as initial conditions, others as consequences of those conditions. From this follows two things that are of central importance for our understanding of what it is to be able to understand, to be able to follow a story of any sort at all. The first is that we cannot take everything that is either explicitly mentioned or implied to a story to be fictional. There must, as it were, be certain law-like assumptions concerning what sorts of consequences should be expected to follow what sorts of initial conditions or situations, however fictional *they* may be. Dragons may not exist, but teeth do and under some circumstances and not others, may be frightening and nasty. Emma Bovary may never have existed, but the sort of society that she was supposed to have existed in did right enough, and certain sorts of behaviour would have been natural to expect, and certain consequences natural to expect from it, so the question can arise "would she have done that?". Even if we are told a story where someone wakes up to find that he is a bed-bug, or a story in which people have a habit of turning into rhinoceroses, the whole world of such a story cannot be fictional and fantastic: if that were so there could be no sense to a question whether what the story says happened *would* have happened or not. Without the possibility of such a question the story, however "realistic" or fantastic, becomes unintelligible and impossible to follow. The second consequence of regarding stories as suppositions is that their intelligibility will depend on our being able to tell *what* element in the story is fictionally supposed and what is not. An author, told that there really are no dragons, that people just do not turn into bed-bugs overnight, can always reply that he has the right to tell any story he chooses, that it is his story, and his story is about these things. But he cannot say this about everything that happens, or is tacitly assumed to be likely to happen, moreover, it is a condition of his story being capable of being followed as a narrative that we should be able to debar him from making this sort of reply concerning some things and not others. If we treat the overt or tacit "once upon a time" as a logical operator, we must be able to tell what aspects of the story it governs and what it does not.

The analogy here with pictures of "fictional" objects would seem to be something like this. A picture of something that is wholly imaginary cannot be *wholly* imaginary: we need to be able at least to construe such a picture as showing us how something or other might be, or how it might look, and this is the same condition as our being able to construe an object (paint on canvas, or whatever it may be) *as* a picture. Suppositions of possible, even if fantastic states of affairs are possible if descriptions and explanations of actual states of affairs are. They are extensions of possibilities. Similarly, pictures of supposed or imagined entities are possible just so long as pictures "from life" are. Moreover, in that the former are possible their possibility depends on our being able to make a distinction between what we merely have to suppose might be "in the story" and something else that depends on our assumptions concerning how things actually are. However, this last condition is by no means an easy one to formulate clearly in the case of pictures.

At first sight it may not seem to be a difficult condition. A picture of a dragon, or of Pegasus, that creature beloved of philosophers, shows us, we could say, how such creatures, if they existed, might look. To paint Pegasus, one paints a horse—and we can recognise how horses look—paints (say) swan's wings, which are familiar enough, and paints them each in such a way that the latter are placed on the back of the former: how else would a winged horse look? The problem is not that a winged horse might equally well be supposed to have the wings of flies, or aeroplanes, but has to do with the idea of "how something looks".

In his paper *On Drawing an Object* Wollheim takes up a question of Wittgenstein's "What is the criterion of the visual experience?" a question which Wittgenstein seemed to answer straightaway, "Well, what would you expect it to be? 'The representation of what is seen' ".[3] Wollheim refers to this as a "stray thought" of Wittgenstein's, but this seems inaccurate, for the remark he refers to is part of a fairly extended complex of remarks concerned with the idea of how things look, how they can be seen in various ways, and the relation of these questions to the function of pictures. That the author of the *Tractatus* should still have been concerned with the question of a relation between picturing and description, and thus with a certain sort of meaning and a certain sort of seeing should not surprise us, and one might, further, compare this remark with two others in *Zettel*:[4]

> I understand this picture exactly, I could model it in clay.—I understand this description exactly, I could make a drawing of it. In many cases we might set it up as a criterion of understanding, that I am able to represent the sense of a sentence in a drawing (I am thinking of an officially instituted test of understanding). How is one examined in map-reading, for example? [And later] How can one learn the truth by thinking? As one learns to see a face better if one draws it.

Perhaps the most significant quotation from this context, however, might be the remark of Wittgenstein's that immediately follows the one Wollheim refers to.

> The concept of a representation of what is seen, like that of a copy is very elastic, and so *together with it* is the concept of what is seen. The two are intimately connected. (Which is not to say that they are alike.) [Wittgenstein's italics.]

It is a familiar observation of painters, and those who have to do with the business of making pictures, that to learn to draw is in some important sense to learn to see. But how are we to take this?

The concept of a criterion can, in this context, be both misleading and somewhat over-impressive. Philosophers have been wont in recent years to use the expression in a somewhat technical sense but more often in what may simply seem to be a precise and technical sense without in fact being so. It seems, however, that in the context of the ideas that Wittgenstein was pursuing all that need be understood is simply a way of finding something out, as in an examination. There may be many ways of testing the same thing and it would be absurd to think that the only way of finding out what someone saw, or how he saw it was by asking him to make a drawing of what he saw. Sometimes it is supposed, on what can seem to be Wittgenstein's warrant, that a criterion of a psychological event is a necessary condition of being able to claim that such an event occurred—clearly, it would be absurd to suppose that only those able to draw are able to see. Wollheim seems to take it, however, that the idea of getting someone to draw what he reports seeing is intended by Wittgenstein to be "an attempt to get behind the observer's words",[5] but in the context of his discussion there seems to be no very strong reason for supposing that this was his intention, for the idea of a representation is not there very clearly contrasted with a description—the thought there seems to be simply that in order to find out what someone's visual experience is we would most naturally ask him to describe what he sees and how he sees it, or, perhaps, get him to draw it for us. Part of that point is that in doing something, making a drawing, describing, or simply exclaiming that *that* is what one sees, one is in different ways expressing thought of the sort that is intimately bound up with what it is to see something at all.

One way of coming to see how this can be so is to look more closely at the kind of activity that can be involved in making a picture of something, even if we do simply construe it as a matter of paying attention to how the thing that one is making can grow to resemble the object that one is attempting to depict. We may imagine someone making a mark on paper or canvas—certainly, if we like with the intention of its being a part of a representation —and then comparing it to what he sees. What he has made, he then matches to what he sees. He will look for resemblances and visual parallels, and watch for their absence. Then, he will adjust what he has done in terms of his intention of maximising such parallels. We could say, if we liked that he proceeds thus until he has got the resemblances between the visual aspects of the two objects before him as close as he can. But to say this would be misleading. On the one hand, even if true it would leave most of what is important in the story out of account, and on the other hand, it is in many cases not even true.

In the first place his perceptual activity is not, as it were, merely looking, but looking *for* something, for resemblances and parallels. If his medium is monochrome pencil, he will not, for instance, look for resemblances in terms of colour, and if his pencil is hard and sharp, he will be unable to find many resemblances in terms of tone and texture, but will find, or fail to find, resemblances in terms of outline, the direction of planes, proportion and so on. If his marks are those characteristic of oil paint, he will look for those kinds of visual characteristics in the object before him. What he is making, and the material constraints on his making that object—the qualities of his medium—will at the same time direct his attention to certain aspects, and not to others in the object before him. How he makes is inevitably how he visually attends. Moreover, his attention will be focused by other things as well which are part of his making. Most painters and draftsmen come equipped to their tasks with whatever they have acquired in terms of past experience and training in how to perform similar tasks. The history of styles of drawing and painting is very largely the history of how painters and draftsmen have come to their tasks so equipped. Much of this is in the form of what can be called "visual clichés". Certain comparatively standardised shapes and types of patterns are in these terms adopted as marks for certain objects, certain sorts of brushstrokes for leaves, for stones or clouds, certain standardised configurations for heads and faces, or horses, and these also will be for the maker of the picture how he attends to the objects seen before him. He will inevitably notice, visually attend to those things that fit such clichés and less to those that fail to. In this sense it is neither a mystical, nor a technical thing to say that those who learn to draw or to paint in a certain style will also see things in terms of that style. Until the work of Stubbs, for example, it seems that painters and draftsmen saw horses differently, more rounded, more barrel-like, constructed in a different way, from how they saw them afterwards.

Clichés can be fought against, and it is also central to the history of style that in this sense new ways of seeing things had to be established by the modification and sometimes total rejection of, such conventional patterns of similarity. Their grip can apply not only to the makers of pictures of course but also to those who use them as ways of finding out how the world, or parts of it, or possible parts of it, look. The process of learning how to see the right matching in new ways of making can take time: as, for example, it took time for most people to see in looking at French Impressionist painting that they were in fact being shown the looks of things and not mere surfaces of paint.

In this sense, to make a picture of anything is, and must be a process of discovery, for if the picture is successful, what has been looked for, resemblances of one sort or another, will have been found. What will have been, to some extent or another, invented as well as discovered, is at the same time new ways of seeing.

But is the task properly accounted for in terms of resemblance? The very idea of visual resemblance in this context is by no means a clear one. How, for example, does an outline pencil drawing of something visually resemble it, even if as accurate as may be? Certainly not by looking the same in any straightforward sense, for we do not in any straightforward sense see outline at all. In some fairly straightforward sense the outline of an object, which is where its visible surface stops and the visible surface of that object it stands in front of begins, is just not a visible thing at all. Or suppose that the drawing goes beyond that to search for planes and the direction of the planes in the object, indicating them by cross hatching and drawing across the "seen" surface of the object. That is not how the object, in some straightforward sense, looks at all, and it would be a strange misunderstanding of the picture to suppose that it invites us to imagine what was seen that way. But, then, what is really meant by this being a "straightforward" sense of "seeing"? What really is the sense in which we do not in fact see the outline of things?

Finally, it is rarely, if ever, true that the maker of a picture of something, however meticulous, continues until he has achieved the closest visual resemblance he can between the object he is making and the object that he is making a picture of. That is not his successful conclusion even if he is simply attempting to achieve a way of showing how he sees the object in terms of how he constructs his picture of it. Yet he may have a successful stopping point nonetheless, which is a conclusion to his activity in making. What can we suppose it to be? Should we say that its conclusion is still in some sense when he has shown us, and perhaps himself, how he sees what he is depicting?

These questions are related to one another. They are also related to two underlying topics: the question of the knowledge of a maker of things and the question of his perception of the world around him. They may usefully be seen in terms of a further question which is a part of that sequence of remarks of Wittgenstein's to which Wollheim's quotation belongs, which is why do we "want to say" that the recognition of something is an "amalgam" of both seeing and thinking?[6]

The general theme of my argument is that of a maker's retrospective discovery of what it is that he is concerned with in his own activity of making. In terms of this the natural question concerning the maker of a representation will be what he may come to know concerning what he is making's being a representation, whether as Wollheim expresses it, the artist, having completed his picture then "comes to know, or that it is only then that he really knows what he saw?"[7] Regarded in one way such a view can certainly sound, as Wollheim says, absurd. Regarded another way it may not even seem so at all. So how should we regard such a claim? Another way of approaching the same question is to ask why the idea that a pictorial representation of something should visually resemble what it represents should have such a hold on us, for it is fairly easy to show how such a view can be related to a certain account of what it is to see, or to perceive, anything.

There is a certain view of perception that runs through whole traditions of philosophy that might be parodied by thinking of ten men standing round a hole in the ground watching five other men digging it. The ten men are "merely observing". Their activity contrasts with that of the men digging in that they are not "doing anything", not that is, engaged in physical activity, though they may well be engaged in considerable mental activity, such as asking themselves what the others are engaged in, interpreting their experience as the experience of five men in a hole, and so on. Observation is not interpretation, on this account, and certainly neither is doing things to or with things. On this account the perceiver is not a physical agent. In that for him to perceive anything at all he must be in some form of contact with the world around him, we must conclude that something is done to him, that he is a patient: the classical version of this doctrine is that in perceiving anything the perceiver "receives impressions".

Now, on this account it is easy enough to see why the very idea of the maker of something, an agent, being at the same time as making an object thereby coming to see something, must seem to be either absurd or misleadingly elliptical for (perhaps) the claim that he puts himself in the way of receiving impressions or the (quite different) claim that he at the same time sets himself to some mental activity that has to do with the interpretation of what he perceives. On either view, to say that the maker of a picture thereby comes to see, or even to know what he sees, must at best be a misleading *façon de parler*, of the sort that writers on the arts are all too prone to. But it is the conception of the perceiver as physically passive that is confused.

It is true enough that merely to look at something will not change it, but as it stands this seems to be a contingent fact about the properties of light. Other forms of perception seem to be different from this. To feel the texture of something, or its weight, it is necessary to touch it and manipulate it. It is hard to see how one could perceive the texture of a piece of moss by touch without affecting the moss in some way. But someone might insist that this is to run together two different aspects of what it is to feel something, namely the physical activity of touching and stroking it, moving or hefting that puts the agent in the way of experiencing some tactile sensation in his fingers or hands, and the sensation itself.[8] It is commonly argued that such perceptual episodes permit the agent to conclude that the object that he is feeling has a certain texture or weight on the basis of an inference from the tactile sensation he has, together with his knowledge of the circumstances in which he has experienced the sensation and thus, on the assumption of certain law-like beliefs that, for example, such and such a sensation of pressure is normally experienced under the circumstances of doing such and such with it so long as its weight is so and so. From such premises and such principles of inference the perceiver then reaches the conclusions he does. Mistakes in perception of this sort can thus be interpreted as either mistakes of inference or mistakes of recognition of the particular tactile sensation. In the large scale of this account, then, perceiving the texture of something is indeed an activity, but in the more precise small scale of the analysis the actual tactile sensation is not. Such a view can seem to bring hefting and feeling into line with seeing. In order to see something, too, it is sometimes necessary to move things about, to pull curtains aside, turn the head or strain the neck, but this is really only a matter of putting oneself into the way of receiving the appropriate sensation: after that the agent is left with a simple matter of sensation and inference.

In his *Autobiography* Collingwood expressed a certain surprise at the fact that his rejection of what, with a somewhat uncritical generality, he called the "Realist" doctrine that what was perceived was not altered by the act of perception inclined his critics to interpret his views as those of an "Idealist" who supposed that what was perceived was always something mental. But the simple doctrine that to perceive the weight or texture of something must affect it supposes nothing of the kind. In fact it supposes quite the reverse. Even if we suppose that the account of tactile perception referred to above is correct, that what is perceived is a tactile sensation, then it will still be the case, since this happens to be how we achieve the situation of having such sensations, that something, normally the object felt, or hefted, is altered. On the other hand, it is not at all clear what would be meant by asking whether the tactile *sensation* is altered or not in such perceptual episodes, so on that account the most natural reply to such a claim surely ought to have been that the question of the thing perceived being altered or not should not arise. To suppose that the only agency in perception could be *mental* agency would thus seem to be plausible at all only on a view of perception that limited the very idea of perception to vision.

Perhaps on this account the correct thing to say is not that we perceive sensations, but that we have them. A traditional way of putting something like this is to talk of the perceiver "receiving impressions". The metaphor is revealing, for it is both one of a certain kind of mechanical causation (an impression is literally a dent) yet seems to permit the idea of a one way causal process. If we adopt the traditional metaphor of the wax tablet, wax tablets are pushed but do not push back. This picture of passivity can be insidious, for it can suggest a train of thought that runs something as follows. What is received by the perceiver from his environment (the "outside" world) is something given by that environment. The perceiver must take it as it comes. An impression cannot be argued with any more than a blow on the head can be. Experience is unarguable because it is the outcome of a physical process: something is and must be "given" in experience. And, of course, that claim (notoriously in the tradition of Empiricism) turns out to be ambiguous. It invites the idea of the phenomenologically "given" in experience. But the sense in which the latter might be said to be given is by no means the same as the sense in which a blow on the head, or an impression in wax or "on the bottom of the eye" is received. The idea of something's being given in experience can also mean, and often turns out to mean, what provides the unarguable experiential premise for a perceptual inference, and *that* is a different matter altogether.

This train of thought which has its modern origin in the Lockian concept of an impression, reaches its familiar terminus in this century in the concept of a sense datum where the conflation of these two senses of something's being "given" often seems to be complete. It is not to my purpose to offer a full account, still less a full criticism, of that doctrine of perception, but it is relevant to note how very closely this way of seeing the matter of perceiving may be related to certain parallel episodes in the history of representational art. It is not quite an accident that the history of a certain kind of painting should have culminated in a style of painting called "impressionism", nor that the theory of impressions in philosophy should be at its most vigorous during that period of European thought during which perspective painting was the dominant form of representational art.

Locke, in explaining how impressions are received by the eye makes a specific reference to this. Explaining how it is that we see such things as convex bodies he says:

> . . . the judgement . . . alters the appearance into their causes; so that, from which truly is variety of shadow or colour collecting the figure, it makes it pass for a mark of figure, and frames to itself the perception of a convex figure and a uniform colour; when the idea we receive from thence is only a plane variously coloured, as is evident in painting.[9]

No passage could provide a better summary of a certain sort of painter's method and theory. It depends on two assumptions, the first being a geometrical model of optics which may also be used to provide the underlying geometry of perspective in painting and the second is a conception of what we might dub a sort of atomistic realism. The eye of the observer may be imagined to be at the apex of a cone of vision in which the seen object is placed. Light from the variously coloured parts of the surface of the object follows the cone and is focused on the retina. We might say that that pattern of light is what is physically received by the eye. But a qualitatively similar effect could have been produced by any other means of projecting the same pattern of light on the retina, for example, that made by the surface of a flat canvas variously coloured in appropriate ways. How the light strikes the eye is the same in each case, but the surface of the second object is flat and not curved: hence recognising the difference is a matter for the judgement "presently, by an habitual custom". The "bare naked perception" which the mind passively receives is interpreted by the judgement, but in the geometrical model, apart from that judgement, there is no difference between the perception of a painting and the real object.

If we turn the model round it can also provide us with the principles of optical perspective in painting, for the perspective cone can be regarded as the visual cone reversed. As objects which we know to be the same size appear to get smaller as they recede from us, the same optical geometry that has light coming towards the eye to an apex, can be applied to the appearances of things. With increasing distance objects appear to occupy proportionately less of the field of view. If we intersect the cone of vision at any point by a device that gives the same input, such as a painted canvas, or copy the input at some point of intersection at right angles to the cone of vision, as we might by colouring a ground glass screen, the eye will still receive the same impressions. We then seem to have a standard of objective measurement of what the eye receives. To apply the test we need only know the underlying geometry and know how to "variously colour" the parts of our canvas or ground glass.

On this account we might then be supposed to have a clear objective test of what someone sees in just that sense in which what he sees is received by the eye. Have we not then a criterion of what is seen in terms of what it is to make a picture? We can reproduce the input.

But there are difficulties with this. The first has to do with what is involved in copying the "variously coloured" patterns that are to issue in patterns of light that will impress themselves on the eye. The same input can certainly not be achieved by the use of monochrome and line, however accurately in perspective. And how small and how finely divided should the coloured patches be? At first sight this may seem to be a simple matter of what is within our technical competence. Perhaps a fine grain colour photograph would be the best to aim for. One thing is sure, however, that is not what Locke could have seen from painting. Perhaps however, as far as that goes all that he need be taken as reporting is that at all events however evenly coloured a sphere may seem to be as we see it, to attempt to reproduce it by the use of an evenly coloured disk will fail. It is not so clear that he was mistaken in that.

The second difficulty for any account of the constraints on the maker of a picture of something is that this sort of procedure of input-reproduction is not what most painters engage in and not what any draftsman could engage in. However, we might suppose, nonetheless, that it is in terms of the possibility of someone's engaging in the sort of exercise that is suggested here that we could at least set up a clear objective test—a criterion—of one sense in which something may be seen, namely that "straightforward" sense in which one does not see outlines and the directions of planes in objects. But is this really so? For in order to apply such a test we have to copy something, we have, in other words to be able to attend to just those aspects of things, just those ways of seeing, that will achieve a similarity, or identity of input. It might be objected that this is not a problem, that the theory of perspective, relying as it does on the well-established geometry of optics and the physiology of the eye can at least provide us with a clear *concept* of what is "straightforwardly" seen. But this is to beg a question. We can only say this so long as we adopt very much the account of perception that Locke is offering us, namely that there *is* a clear difference in perception between what the eye "passively" receives and how the "judgment presently . . . alters the appearances into their causes". This requires that we can in fact identify the former as distinct from the latter. To discount that issue is to conflate the idea of something being passively received as a blow on the head may be and its being the unarguable data of experience. There seems to be no justification for doing so.

We are thus bound to return again to the fact that a picture, however closely it may be required to resemble its topic is still something *made* to do so.

It is important to note that the system of perspective is one among many projective systems that have been and are used in drawing. The idea of a projective system is easy enough to state in general terms and very difficult to analyse in all its ramifications, but in its simplest terms we may regard it as a system of rules or principles which permits us to say of one complex object and another that the parts of the former may be mapped onto the parts of the latter. The simplest example of such a relationship is that of two systems being isomorphic with one another in the sense that each element in one corresponds to a unique element in the other: unfortunately it is not applicable to the relation of a picture to its topic, since it is a relation that is both symmetrical and at the same time transitive. Were the relation of a picture to what it depicts to be regarded in this way we would be able to conclude both that the object depicted equally depicted its own picture and that two pictures of the same object were pictures of each other. We might attempt a weaker account than this in which by some rule or principle such that two structures may be regarded so that one is a projection of the other so long as some identifiable parts or groups of parts of one system may be unambiguously paired with similar parts or groups of parts of the other. Since it is possible to group the parts of any complex in different ways, such a relation is no longer transitive, but it is still symmetrical, and thus still raises problems for how it is that a drawing may be said to represent its topic. If we take a drawing to be, as not all drawings are, a flat surface intended to represent a flat or solid object, we can imagine the system of projection being defined in terms of lines running from points in the drawing to corresponding points in the object. We may then distinguish different systems of this sort in terms of the relation of those imaginary lines to one another. Thus in what is called "orthographic projection" the lines are parallel to one another, as a shadow of an object may be thrown on a wall or a screen by the sun when the screen is at right angles to the direction of the sun from it to the object. In the case of perspective drawing the corresponding lines converge at that imaginary vanishing point in the picture at which an object will have diminished beyond the point of visible appearance. All sorts of different geometrical constructions may, on this account, be adopted to classify various systems of drawing—the lines running parallel, diverging or converging in various ways, or lying at various angles to the plane of the picture. But even such an account runs into certain difficulties, even though they may be safely ignored in certain sorts of practice. The difficulties are very much the same as those involved in supposing that a picture can represent its topic by resembling it, namely that as with resemblance, none of them account for the asymmetry of representation, namely that a picture of an apple is not itself pictured by the apple: lines of projection have two directions.

None the less, something of this sort is essential to the very idea of representation. A representation of one thing by another must at the very least be a matter of structural parallel. A viceroy represents a queen by occupying an analogous position in a corresponding political structure, a representative represents his constituents by occupying a position for them in a structure of debate. Similarly, to see a picture or map or model as a representation of something is to see the part of the system that is the map, picture or model as similarly structured to the system they represent so that both the parts may stand for parts in the topic and in doing so that the topic has, or may be seen as having such a structure is revealed. A model, picture or map shows how things are or might be by showing how they can be understood as related. It is a matter of elements standing proxy for things in so far as they may be seen as a structure. A minimal way of putting this is to say that *only* a complex or a unit seen as a part of a complex can represent, for the perception that one thing does represent another is the perception of a common structure that in consequence permits the recognition of part of the model being able to be seen as corresponding to a part in its topic. Perhaps the most important consequence for one who (like the author of the *Tractatus*) sought an account of significance in general in the concept of representation is that no simple unit within a system of significance can have a significance on its own.

This is the lesson we can apply to the matter of making pictures, for to make a picture is essentially, on this account to make a pattern, a structure or, as we have seen, a design. It is only in terms of his being able to do this that he can construct something that is able to represent something at all. Designing is in this sense also presupposed in picturing. His attention must be to the design he is making if it can be to what he is representing. But then he is bound to attend to the object of his representation *as* comparably ordered.

In the light of this we might view the sort of thing that Locke has to say in another way. Let us imagine a painter of the kind he tacitly refers to engaged in his task. Before him he has not only an object to be depicted, but also paints, brushes and canvas. As he paints the marks that he makes come to be seen by him as standing for the variously coloured parts of the surfaces of things. A certain patch of pigment is seen to correspond to a patch of seen colour, but it cannot do so on its own. His search for those unit patches of colour that can be seen in the object is a form of attention to how he places the colour on his canvas. Locke's insistence that how objects are presented to the eye is contrary to how we judge them to be "as may be seen in painting" corresponds quite closely to a certain stylistic tradition in representative art, with its attendant recipes for representation: "paint what you see, not what you think that you see." A shiny evenly coloured object such as a blue vase may be reported by an honest observer with perfect truth to be evenly blue, but that is not how a painter would, in this tradition, paint it. What he puts on the canvas before him is a pattern of brush strokes of modulated colour and tone that together add up to how the vase looks. To paint the area in the picture that corresponds to the vase an even blue would not be to paint how it appears. The object is shadowed by other colours, reflects and takes up the light from its surroundings, shows to the attentive eye a complex of appearances. The painter produces a similar complex. But it would be a mistake to take even this too literally.

Sometimes the painter engaged in such an exercise may compare the colour of the paint on the canvas he is working on with the detailed patches of colour he attends to in the object, but he does not only do that. Patch for patch the colours may not even match. His painting may be more blue than the object, have a narrow range of colour or a less narrow one. He may still succeed, and succeed in terms of just the sort of pictures that could be regarded as most clearly representational in the sense of this account.

The painting will still work if the relationships are right. His modulation of colour across the surface of the vase in his painting may be a modulation of a different colour from that of the seen object, even a broader or narrower modulation, but so long as it is possible to recognise a parallel pattern of colour the picture will still show how the object may be seen. It need not, of course, be a correspondence in terms of colour at all. A line drawing that presents outlines, or defines the direction of planes, models the object, even how it is seen, by replicating not the parts of the manifold of appearances, but the relations between them. In no way does such a drawing, or most paintings, look like what they represent in the sense that they could be mistaken for their appearances: the sense in which they look like them is the sense in which they can be seen to show a structure in how they look, and how something looks, just as how something is may be regarded as structured in various sorts of ways.

That tradition of painting, then, which most conforms to the model of representation that Locke refers to may be regarded as a way of seeing the world, not by any means an inaccurate way, but by no means the only accurate way. It is noteworthy how far it can be possible to read those philosophical accounts of perception that claim that "what we really see" are sense data as if they were instructions for seeing the world in terms of a certain sort of painting, for we may pay attention to just those detailed patches of colour before us as if what we saw were complexes of variously patterned colours and shapes. There seems to be no reason to conclude from this that this is what is "given" in experience.

Representation being what it is—on the most minimal account—it must follow that in one way or another *any* picture is atomistic, for any picture at all can be divided up into progressively smaller areas such that at some point the necessary pictorial structure will be lost. This can be discovered empirically in any painting or reproduction of a painting. A small area of a large picture may be seen as a detail—a figure or the eye of a figure—but there will come a point where such a division will yield only something that can be seen as a patch of pigment. What that area will be will depend on the particular picture concerned. This is a fact well known to the designers of jig-saw puzzles, difficult puzzles being those whose pieces are mostly below this "pictorial mesh" size. For those who enjoy that sort of thing, part of the interest in playing with such puzzles derives from the way in which a picture can seem to rather magically emerge from what seem to be insignificant units. The physical size of such units may be called the grain of the picture. It may be objected at this point that there might surely be, at least in theory, pictures which have as it were infinitely fine grain, where one might continue to magnify the details indefinitely, as perhaps with a "perfect" photograph. Certainly photographs can be made which are capable of providing pictorial information at quite remarkable small scale, so why not indefinitely? One reply to this might be that any photographic emulsion must eventually show its grain, at least at its molecular level, but such a reply would miss the point. For photography plays an interesting role in the account of perception and representation we have been considering in that, given the optical and geometrical theory of perspective in this account, a camera may be regarded as replicating the physical situation of a normal eye. In this sense would not a perfectly fine grained photograph provide us a picture of the world as it can be seen in all its detail? If such a picture must have a pictorial mesh is this not another way of saying that perception itself must have such a mesh?

In fact ordinary visual perception does seem to have a mesh and a relatively coarse one at that: it is perfectly possible to attend to a coloured patch in one's field of vision in such isolation from other such objects that it does not appear as a part of anything in particular. It can be tempting to regard such percepts as the uninterpreted "given" in experience. Philosophers such as Russell seem to have regarded the world in just such a way, adopting for this purpose the language of perspective painting. For Russell it somehow seemed to be the most natural thing in the world to say that material objects were logical "constructions" of such perceptual atoms built together in terms of the principles of perspective. On such a view it then becomes a relevant question to ask whether the relative coarseness of our normal perceptual mesh depends simply on the fact that, unlike ideally perfect cameras, we do not have "microscopical eyes". But this is again to confuse two different issues, a causal, optical, theory and an account of attention.

We are not all painters, but we are all *attenders,* and what paintings and drawings can show us is how to attend. For the various ways in which we can attend to things, including how we may attend below an interpretive mesh, can be varied in all sorts of ways. One may attend to a patch of asphalt as an even extended area of grey, or as a textured surface, or as a coloured space between other objects. One may attend to the surface of an untidy desk as a mass of paper or as an array of papers, or as a modulated area of colour. If a missing sheet of paper is on such a desk, before my eyes, yet I fail to see it, to notice it even though I may have been looking right at it, this is because of the ways in which I have attended to what was before me, and this is a matter of how I see the organisation of what is before me. In this sense there is indeed a close connection between what it is for something to be presented to me in experience and what it is for something to be represented to me by a picture. Russell's (not very explicit) analogy of the structure of perception with the ways in which a picture works was not mistaken, what was mistaken was the way in which it was drawn.

In certain kinds of painting, but not in others, the maker of the picture may adopt the stylistic tactic of matching the pictorial mesh-size to the average size of his brush strokes, or just below it, so that each smallest significant detail of the picture roughly corresponds to a passage of paint application. There can be a tendency to associate a certain sort of realism with this kind of technique. This is not inevitable; in certain sorts of painting—that of early Renaissance "primitives", for example—the average brush stroke size is well below the pictorial mesh, while in other sorts of painting commoner in the present century—what is often regarded as expressionist non-abstract painting—the brush strokes tend to be considerably larger than the smallest significant detail, so that a whole breast may correspond to a whole sweep of applied paint, and a part of the former to a part of the latter. The communicative effect of such devices can be to relate the observer's attention in different ways to the evidences of the physical act of painting and what is shown to have been seen, or may be supposed as having been seen. How the maker of the picture made his picture becomes a way of seeing how he attended. In the former of these stylistic types his pictorial construction—how the materials were put together—partially reenacts the pattern of his attention, and the attention to a possible, imagined, seen object he invites from us. He is at the same time depicting an object and his attention to how the unorganised units of his attention could be seen to be related. If we regard the world in terms of a theory of impressions or sense-data, his way of painting is in this sense impressionistic. Impressionism is, not surprisingly, the culmination of a certain sort of search for realism, for the accurate record of what is seen in terms of a tacit assumption concerning what seeing is. The second stylistic tendency can have the effect, as it were of presenting an account of what is seen in terms of whole objects—the *minima divisibilia* of perception are seen as things and not as percepts: it is as if there is nothing to be seen below the level of identifiable things in space. In the latter case seen objects are, as it were, shown to us in terms of the physical activity of laying down, manipulating and constructing physical objects that are composed of paint. In so far as we can regard the construction of a pattern or organisation of material as a testimony to the exercise of the thought of a maker, an expression of his thought in making, we are thus led to see the depicted objects in terms of that expression of practical thought with materials.

It is hard to offer even such a schematic summary of pictorial styles for ways of drawing. And it must be remembered that drawing and painting are not fundamentally different ways of depicting things. The painter will draw with his brush. The main difference between drawing and painting—a difference of degree only—is that in a drawing, such as a drawing that uses line alone, what is put down on the paper or canvas is not marks that stand for relata in a representational structure, but marks that, such as outlines, hatching that indicate the direction of planes and so on, indicate relata in terms of signs for relationships. But here again we can make similar distinctions, between pictures that indicate objects in terms of a continuous calligraphic line, those that indicate in terms of line the limits of what tends to be the smallest significant units within the picture, and those which construct linear patterns below such a level. Again, ways of attending and ways of making are drawn together.

How, then, can we approach the question of what way we may regard a drawing as a criterion of what is seen, and what might this really show us concerning perception and judgement?

The symmetry between a representation and what is represented cannot in fact be ignored. It needs however, to be seen for what it is. An apple is indeed not a picture of that object that represents it, but it is the case that in so far as a picture is successful how the apple is seen by the maker of the picture, and, if successful in communicating what it is concerned with to the observers of the picture, how it may be seen by them. (Resemblance of visual input is only one way in which this may be thought of. The nearest one can approach to an example of such resemblance would be in the case of *trompe l'oeil* painting of the sort that approaches the condition of actually being mistaken for the object it represents, but even in such cases, while we might very well suppose the picture to be mistaken for its object, it is still much less easy to imagine how the objects depicted might be mistaken for their own picture. To achieve such an effect it would be necessary to place them in such a way that the could be seen from a particular point in space, for that extreme sort of representational device depending as it does on a static optical model, requires that what can be represented should be confined to how an object is seen from one particular point.)

What the maker of a picture attends to in making it is then, not the object he sees, but rather *how* he sees it. His retrospective attention to the processes of his design, to the constraints on the choices and decisions that he makes as he works it out as he goes along are at the same time constraints on his attention to how he sees the object he is depicting. To attend thus is both a form of understanding and a form of perception. It is that which a successful picture shows. When a picture is an artefact (in the sense in which a photograph which, since automatically produced is not designed as made) that understanding and attention may also be regarded as the outcome of a process of making. It is this that such pictures communicate.

Wittgenstein asked how one could learn the truth by thinking, and he answered his own question by replying that one might to do in that way in which one might come to see a face better by drawing it. The underlying thesis here is surely that this form of coming to learn something is a process of construction. His suggestion is all of a piece with his account of establishing a mathematical truth[10] by the *construction* of a proof. He suggested in the same context that a test of understanding a picture might be that I could model it in clay, or of a description that I could make a drawing of it. This points to an important sense in which one may come to understand anything at all: in this sense to understand something is to make something of it, a representation of it. And this suggestion seems to go well beyond the mere claim that one could simply come to discover that someone understood something, for the very making itself is a process of understanding. To make a representation of something is to make an analogical construction out of units: to see it as such an analogue is to come to understand how it holds together, its construction, its design, how the parts may be understood in terms of the whole. In accord with this general view a picture of something, such as a drawing or a painting is finished when the maker has shown himself, as well as any others who may come to look at it, how it is that he sees it. In just the same way to make a model of something is, if successful, to have come to understand its order, how the parts belong together in terms of the whole, and this is what we might perhaps term "maker's knowledge",[11] but perhaps misleadingly, for the point is not that the maker knows more, or better, than another how the picture, or the pictured object hangs together, but that the process by which he comes to know this is the very same *process* as his making. His coming to know, or to understand what he sees is his making the picture. This is how a drawing, or for that matter a description may be a criterion of what is seen—to realise what one sees is to realise, to make a reality of, what represents it.

To make a successful picture of how one sees something should not be understood in terms of achieving a perfect visual match between the picture and its topic, for in the sense of "see" that is relevant here, an object may be seen in many different ways. Moreover, they may differ from one another without it being the case that any one such way of seeing an object need be mistaken or "wrong". The easiest way of showing why this is so is, perhaps, to point out that in so far as a picture is a representation it has certain logical features that are common to all representational systems, such as for example, maps or models. Maps or models may show us how things are, or how they might be, while at the same time being highly simplified and selective. A map of the London Underground System may be accurate enough without including information about every turn and twist of the line, still less about every noticeable feature of the railway or the stations, yet still truly show how the system is ordered, what station has to be reached before another, what stations are or are not junctions and so on. In general, any map or model may be used to show what is the case (may show something that truly is) while being very much simpler than its topic. On the other hand any such model will always show something false if it is more detailed than its topic, for then it will contain elements that purport to represent what is not present in reality. This is why in general the relation of some representation to its topic is a logically asymmetrical one, for A may truly represent B (be an accurate model of B) while being simpler than B—which is normally the case—while B can never be a similar representation of A under such circumstances.

The situation is quite different in the case of the relation between a picture of an object and *how it is seen,* for how an object is seen may both be a selection of the object's features or aspects (and still, to that extent accurate) in this case how the object is seen cannot be answered separately from how the picture is constructed: the maker of a picture in so far as the picture was a successful exercise of thought in making, came to see the object in making a representation of it. There is much truth in that idiom that expresses the claim that someone saw or thought of something in a certain way that says that that is how "he represented it to himself". We do not need to be expert painters and draftsmen to be able to do that.

Notes

1 cf. my "Representation and Conceptual Change" in *Philosophy and the Arts* ed. G. Vesey, Royal Institute of Philosophy Vol. 6., 1971/2, Macmillan, 1973.
2 *Art and Illusion* Phaidon Press 1960 p. 99 ". . . always, I contend, making will come before matching, creation before reference."
3 *Philosophical Investigations,* p. 198.
4 cf. *Zettel,* Blackwell, 1967, pp. 245–55.
5 *op. cit.,* p. 4.
6 *Philosophical Investigations,* p. 197.
7 *op. cit.,* p. 5.

8 See, for example, Armstrong's account in *Bodily Sensations*, Routledge, 1962.

9 Locke, *Essay Concerning Human Understanding*, Bk. II, Ch. 9, sec. 8.

10 cf. *Remarks on the Foundations of Mathematics*.

11 The idea of "maker's knowledge" is discussed by Jaakko Hintikka in *Practical Reason* (*op cit.*) pp. 84–102 and related to Vico's claim that "the rule and criterion of truth is to have made it". The view that this is a special kind of knowledge is attacked in the same volume by J. L. Mackie. As they stand Mackie's criticisms seem to hit their target, but they do so because the idea of "knowledge" is the wrong one in this context: it belongs, as it were, to the "statics" of the philosophy of mind. What is required is the "dynamic" idea of a maker's thought in what he does.

CONCLUSION

THE central idea in the foregoing is that in the case of most making, and of all designing and composing, we have to do with a process of discovery. Broadly speaking, two kinds of discovery are involved, one having to do with what we might call, with some hint of a pun, the material conditions of his achieving an intended result, the other to do with the agent's own understanding of his own ends. In each case the important point is that such discoveries on the part of the maker can only be made in terms of his attention to the artefact that he is bringing into being as it emerges before him, or else to a clear and more or less vivid imagination on his part of how that artefact can come to be by modifying its present state. (In this latter way, for instance, a painter may be able to visualise the next steps in his making of his picture—for him to continue working successfully what he visualises must at least be the *next* steps, and where he cannot do this he must needs, and fortunately usually can, pay attention to his own next act in painting.) In this sense a bad maker of something is one who does not quite know what he is doing, sometimes, but not always in the sense that he does not know what he is setting out to achieve, but *always* in the sense that he is not paying *attention* to what he is doing.

This concept of attention is thus equally central; what the bad or unsuccessful maker is not paying attention *to* is, in all of the simplest and most straightforward cases, not something *mental*, as it might be what he wants to achieve (that which he intends) but something material, the not-yet-finished artefact that he is working on. To be sure, that object is attended to, seen, in a certain way, according to a certain aspect, is seen as something which with his co-operation may emerge or develop in a certain way, but it is still something, something already made and done, that is seen in that way, something that is not merely imaginary. A large part of the discipline that constrains a maker's attention and that practice that springs from it derives simply from his having to realise this, that even a partly finished artefact is an object, which thereby imposes its "objective" constraints on his attention. The apparently rather mysterious sense in which it is sometimes held that the maker of something, especially something like a work of art, a poem or a picture, makes an "objective correlative"[1] of something that he thinks or feels may in this way be pinned down to this not very mysterious fact that a maker of something is a maker of *something*: if his activity "objectifies" something mental,[2] it does so because what is made is an object which he himself may attend to or fail to attend to, but which can none the less stand independently of his attention or his thought.

The inattentive workman who fails to keep his mind on the job, is failing to attend to the job in hand in that sense of "job" which we might call the artisan's sense in which a job is something that can be left on the bench or set aside at the end of the day's work. One way of identifying the polemic that runs through my discussion of a maker's thought is that intellectuals in general—and in this context, philosophers in particular—have tended to neglect the central relevance of this sense of a job in hand in thinking of intelligent and intelligible actions and projects. It is to this idea of a job in hand,—rooted in those mundane cases where the job may be quite literally "in hand"—that we need to turn if we are to start at the ground floor of any enquiry into the idea of practical thinking however much the upper stories of the grand edifice of "practical reason" may be reserved for such un-artisan activities as moral or legal speculation and judgement.

The most primitive and elementary picture we can have of an inventive maker's thought in what he does is both as simple and as complex as what we may observe in watching a child making sandcastles. If we note the result of his activities alone there may be very little to tell us in the piled heaps of sand that he leaves behind him for the tide to wash away whether he was making sand castles or merely playing around with heaps of sand, very little to tell us whether he was mucking about or making, for small children are rarely very good at building when they start out. None the less, the least percipient parent can normally tell from how the child behaves which of these things he is doing. The child is seriously making something when he attends to what he is achieving in a certain way. He stands back from it to see how it looks, to see if it is going right, what it is turning into, how it is failing to develop in one way or another, how it may be emerging as something of which he can be proud or persist in disappointing him by falling down just as it is about to *be* something worth identifying as a castle or a harbour. In the same way his idea of what he is after emerges from, or in, his attention to what he is making. We can often see this going on from the way we can observe how he concentrates on his work.

To be sure, goals may well precede the activities of bringing things about as a child may arrive on a beach with the fixed prior intention of making something highly specific, often with absurdly over-ambitious plans for his architectural feats in sand. But this is certainly not always so, and even where it is so we should be careful not to be misled by too simple a picture of an agent's succeeding or failing to achieve a goal he has set himself. There are, for instance, those terrible occasions where the sand builder rages in inarticulate frustration at what seems to others to be a perfectly innocent piece of beach. To the maker it seems otherwise: he wants so much to produce something that will be splendid and complete, the perfect sand-castle, only just what that might be is so elusive. But not only does the sand not do what it should, but because of that one cannot *say*, because one cannot *quite* imagine, just what it is that it should be doing. The frustration derives from the fact that one cannot "realise" one's intention in two quite different ways. One cannot quite know, quite realise, just what one does want, and one cannot do that because one cannot bring what one wants about—it can be that way round. The worst thing that can happen is for some helpful adult to kindly interfere by suggesting that if only one tells him just what it is that one is trying to do he may be able to help, armed as he is with his greater knowledge of the ways of sand, for that is just what one cannot tell him. So the implied charge is that one is being silly, complaining that one cannot get what one does not even know that one wants. But it *isn't* a false hunger that one feels, only one cannot *show* that it isn't. To be trapped like this is to be trapped by the myth of means and ends.

On better days it is as if the castle builder and the sand have a kind of dialogue together. The materials shape themselves as they are shaped by the maker, and as they are shaped so they not only conform to what he wants but can be seen as conforming more and more to how he comes to see how they might be. The process of imagination is itself formed by its being something that is not imagined that is seen in a particular way. If sand is seen as a castle it is still sand that is seen that way. With different materials the castle, however much in the eye of the beholder, would be imagined differently. Of course it is possible enough to imagine castles or anything else, really in the air, without being engaged in making anything at all. I am not arguing that imagination cannot be exercised except in terms of the practical activities of making things (generally, and quite deliberately, I have avoided the concept of imagination *as such*). But what I am claiming is that the practical activities of making things and of inventing and designing things are essentially like this and that making is the most basic of all our practical activities. The "standard" simpler models that we tend to think of when we reflect on the nature of thought and practice are sophisticated simplifications to which at best our most organised and careful activities may sometimes conform. If we fail to recognise this such standard models can only be over-simplified and sophistical.

At the other end of the scale from making sand-castles are those highly sophisticated activities of making of the sort that most normally get the attention of philosophers. I mean such things as making, composing, thinking out, and inventing explanations, theories, proofs, and, of course, even exercises in philosophy. Such things, however "abstract" are artefacts and are the outcome of processes of making. Can an understanding of more mundane processes of making help us to learn anything about these sorts of "artefacts" and about how they come to be?

Perhaps such a question should not find its place at the conclusion of such an enquiry as this but should have been posed at the beginning. However, the omission is deliberate, for it is the "un-abstract" "unsophisticated" sorts of making that philosophers have tended to neglect. It is, moreover, an omission that is not part of this enquiry to remedy, even though there may be strong grounds for supposing that it is in these areas that most of the most pressing philosophical work needs to be done. We do not know enough, and we could attempt to find out more about *how* such intellectual artefacts, such "constructions" get made. As writers such as Hanson[3] have rightly pointed out, philosophers of Science have traditionally tended to concentrate their attention on the question of the justification and testing of scientific theories rather than on the *philosophical* (as opposed to historical) question of the *kind* of thought that can be involved in their coming to be as products of human intellectual activity, and, while since Hanson made that claim a considerable amount of work has been put in in an effort to remedy the defect, it is still perhaps not wholly clear that the necessary preliminary work has been done to isolate the relevant philosophical questions—partly because of the difficulty that many writers seem to find in escaping from the pull of the static concepts of knowing and believing towards the more dynamic concepts of inventing, designing, of coming to a conclusion, of working things out. (The problems of making are not concerned with makers' *knowledge* but with the nature of his thought in what he is doing.)

To show something of the shape of what I have been concerned with in the most general terms it may be necessary to make the implications of the foregoing paragraph a little more clear: a brief attempt to do so will have to stand as my conclusion —which can at best be an indication of unfinished business.

Where what is made is not, as a sand-castle or a painting is, a material object made of "stuff" and "things" but is an "intellectual" object such as a theory, an explanation, a proof, or a piece of philosophical analysis, the central element of discovery shows itself in much the same way. But here we reach a difficulty which it might be felt I should have faced at the outset of my account. The difficulty is that this fact can very easily seem to be perfectly trivial, for to "make", compose or construct any of these things involves the solving of *problems*, and, as J. L. Mackie[4] puts it, "it is absurd to say . . . 'I know the solution to this problem so I shall now proceed to solve it' ", absurd, since, obviously, to *seek* to solve a problem is *not* to have solved it. But then, no cases of making anything that are a matter of quite slavishly following someone else's or one's own prior instructions, all involve problem solving, so it may be felt that all I have had to say concerning the element of discovery in making collapses into this truism—problem solving just is like that, so why should we need to make heavy weather of the matter?

A truism, is, of course, true, but its danger can be that its very truth can mask any deeper issues. The problem has been to bring them out. We can illustrate this by considering that form of problem solving that will be most familiar to philosophers, namely, doing philosophy itself.

There are, perhaps as many views about the essential nature of philosophical problems as there are, or have been, philosophers, it being part of the essential nature of the matter of philosophy to contest its own nature, yet one might still find fairly substantial agreement among philosophers of all kinds that at the very least an important part of their business is concerned with laying bare, examining and criticising the underlying assumptions that we may make in the course of our every-day or specialist thinking and judging. It is normally with how we are to interpret this very weak and general claim that the difficulties arise. It is as if the most elusive of all philosophical questions was, what is an implicit or underlying assumption or belief—or merely, "way of thinking"—and what is it to unearth such a thing? One possible answer to such a question might be to suppose, as it sometimes seems as if Kant does, that underlying all our normal thought and judgement lies a system of beliefs of greater and greater generality (the greater the generality the deeper one digs) whose relation to each other is not unlike that of more or less general laws in a fully worked out system of scientific explanation: as if we might say that as any particular perceptual judgement were a little science, the largest science of all was the whole body of rational thought. The two pictures of thought belong together. It is as if the form of our judgements was constrained by our convictions of "what makes sense" to assert or deny, and as if those convictions were capable of being ordered into a "conceptual system" whose form was that of a "meta-physical" theory concerning what general sorts of things must be or might be or could not be, and thus what less general kinds of things there are or could be.

If we are inclined to see the topics of the philosophical enterprise in this way, we will be naturally faced with two further questions about it. One will be whether there is in fact, or could be proved to be by philosophical argument, just one such all-embracing system for any rational thinker, or whether there may be many varieties for different people, or different societies or different historical periods. If we are inclined to adopt the second view (perhaps on the grounds that the relevant philosophical proofs, the "transcendental deductions", could never be successful)[5] it will be natural to suppose that there may be two sorts of philosophical exercises open to us, namely that of simply describing or exhibiting what some people's, a particular person's or a society's "metaphysical" beliefs actually are or alternatively, that of proposing to them that they might well adopt others.[6] Hence, the second question we will be faced with concerning our own activities as philosophers will be which of these two things we may find ourselves doing. The distinction is as easy to state as that between what is and what ought to be, or may be recommended to be—and as difficult to imply in practice. And this is so whether or not we believe that "transcendental arguments" can be successful.

The reason is that while it is perfectly clear sometimes that we may have very good grounds for saying of someone—or even to someone—that he is committed to, or working with some fundamental belief of which he may not be aware, indeed, that we *must* sometimes be able to say this, it is by no means so clear a matter in what sense we are "telling" him this. We may be able to argue, for instance, that someone's insistence that there just could not be a disembodied being (or that there might be) commits him to certain assumptions concerning bodies, persons and so on, on which he has not reflected. But does he believe these things, or are we telling him that he better had? To put the matter another way, if some (or even all) philosophical analysis is descriptive in this way then it must be as it were a form of intellectual anthropology,[7] but then such an enterprise will encounter the problems of anthropological enquiry in the field, for it will always *be* "in the field", and will be concerned with telling the subjects of one's observations what those observations are. Most often it is the philosopher's own thought and belief that provides his subject matter.

For it is hard to see how the examination of a belief can leave that belief unaltered. If old Mrs. Smith, who all her life has believed that what she learnt in Sunday School was literally and metaphorically Gospel truth is asked to report as innocently and honestly what it is that she does believe, it may be that in doing so she realises for the very first time her total conviction that she can look forward to meeting her husband in Heaven, raises a problem for her Biblical reading that marriages are not given in Heaven: her efforts to *report* what it is that she does believe will itself alter what it is that she believes. But then is she reporting at all?

But perhaps we should ask, rather what it is to say that she is *believing*, not because we may suspect her of dishonesty (the problem exists because she is *not* dishonest) and not because of the notion of her *unconsciously* believing either, but because the problem *what* she believes that she may begin by not knowing the solution to (the problem that she starts to solve by starting to tell us) itself shifts. It is not just that when she sets out to solve the problem (or when we do in philosophically examining our own beliefs) she does not yet know the solution, it is that by the same token she (and we in the analogous predicament) do not yet know the *problem*. The child who does not know the solution to the problem how to get the sand to do what he intends at the same time does not fully know what it *is* that he intends; knowing the problem goes along with knowing the solution, and does not precede it.

The point of the analogy between philosophical problem solving and making is then this, that making something clear, spelling something out, exhibiting an analysis, is making something that we can set apart from ourselves and pay attention to in just the same way that the child who makes a castle on the beach has made something that he may either attend to or turn away from. What is involved is *ex*pression in both cases, the production of something apart, to that extent, however intimately related to a process of thought, something new and different, an artefact. As far as the philosophical exercise goes we could express the matter by saying that even the most scrupulously "descriptive" clarification of what underlies a pattern of thought must necessarily extend it. (In this way, even if Kant had been right in supposing that his demonstration of the underlying categories of rational thought were the only possible demonstration, or if another philosopher should rightly suppose so of his analysis, it would still be the case that his account would be an extension of thought and belief, not a "mere" account of it.)

One possible way of taking this line of reflection further could be to raise a sceptical doubt concerning the very idea of what it is to have a fundamental underlying belief of which one is not fully aware; and indeed it is an obscure and difficult enough idea on any account. Its obscurity goes along with the obscurity in the closely related idea that, for instance, one who simply recognises something, something that is familiar to him such as a variety of tree or a potsherd of a certain type that could only be recognised by another after a long period of careful reflection and inference, unconsciously and rapidly infers to a conclusion that the other reaches slowly and painfully, for surely it is not that he travels the same road swiftly and silently that the other travels with toil, but that he has no need of travelling such a road at all. Or again, we might ask why, in the case of all behaviour and thought different from our own—and for that reason mysterious—questions of underlying beliefs should arise at all. I can vividly recall that as a child I was quite certain, whenever accused of some crime by my parents, that only my teddy bear understood me, but what did I believe about such things? Did I believe that a thing of fur and sawdust was capable of silent reflection? Surely not, but then, what did I really believe? Surely, the right thing to say is that questions of that sort do not arise, that we could in principle have no way of getting a grip on them. Such a line of scepticism would indeed be all of a piece with my earlier objections to that pattern of philosophical analysis that sees the thought involved in an action always in terms of the agent's reasons for performing it, for it is not difficult to see in each case an obsessive concern with the idea of *justification* taking up the whole area of that of thought in what we do. But that is not the moral I wish to conclude with.

The moral is rather this. As far as the philosophical enterprise itself goes we might put it that philosophy cannot simply consist in conclusions. Philosophers sometimes object to that way of conducting the business that leaves all the rough work on the page and which cannot conclude with a clear claim that for such and such reasons this is so. By those standards the foregoing exercise is untidy work. But any extension of thought must be a process. It can stand or fall accordingly, only in terms of being able to show the way in which the process moves, by being able to show where it has come from, and by what stumbling and what erasures sometimes all one may be able to show is how one might move further. In this sense a conclusion can only be an invitation. It is not for me to judge whether the invitation is worth while.

This is not to endorse metaphysical relativism. It might seem that if we deny a view that holds out as a possible goal for the philosophical enterprise that it may be able to lay bare *the* underlying structure of rational thought we should be forced to adopt as the alternative that there may be all sorts of mutually closed "conceptual frameworks" (for different societies, ages, or stages in"conceptual development") between which we are in no position to make a rational choice. Such a view would indeed involve a doctrine of metaphysical despair, but in fact these alternatives do not exhaust the possibilities and they each make the same implausible assumption that we can unambiguously "describe" an underlying pattern of assumptions and presuppositions in such a way that we can say that those assumptions are the ones that belong to a given (or any) way of thinking. To claim as I do both that we cannot in any clear sense do this is to deny both of these alternatives, and to claim as I do that in the course of our agreements, disagreements, refutations and discussions we may change and develop our underlying presuppositions as we go along (typically, but not exclusively, as we continue the enterprise as philosophers) is merely to claim *that*. In denying a clear sense to the idea of a metaphysical final solution there is no need at all to suppose that anything goes, that one set of underlying assumptions or conceptual presuppositions is as good as another. Indeed it is to claim quite the reverse, for it is in being prepared to deny just that that we do develop our ways of thinking. (The analogy with the representational enterprise of a painter is, if loosely, that his struggle to develop new ways of seeing is made possible because he works with the twin convictions that there may be many different and successful ways of seeing the world or items in it while at the same time there may be all sorts of *failures* in the attempt to depict the way things can be seen. Together these assumptions amount to the conviction that there is an objective reality to be depicted that imposes its own discipline on what he does.)

In a famous passage in the *Journals* Kierkegard seems to draw what appear to be relativistic conclusions from the thought that, "It is perfectly true as philosophers say, that life must be understood backwards. But they forget that other proposition that it must be lived forwards. And if one thinks over that proposition it becomes more and more evident that life can never really be understood in time simply because at no particular moment can I find the necessary resting-place from which to understand it—backwards."[8] If I understand this mysterious passage correctly it seems to invite two replies. On the one hand, our "resting place", our vantage point from which to "understand backwards" is how we attend to what we *now* suppose and believe, whatever we might speculate we might subsequently suppose. It is difficult to see what we could have or wish otherwise. On the other hand, and perhaps more radically, that just as attending to the behaviour of sand *itself*, along with any conception of what he wants to do or thinks that he is doing constrains a child's construction of his sand-castle, so we similarly always have a real world as our constraint. Of course we can't replace that by a *theory*, however well-wrought—we would be in a pretty sort of a pickle if we could, and of course *that* in no possible way implies that we should abandon our conviction that the world is real enough. The very idea of a development of thought requires such a realist premise. We may think about the world in a variety of ways but it is not by that token a world of thought, still less of a variety of thoughts. Making, whether of things or theories, is always in this sense a matter of attending to the material conditions of its activity whatever else may be involved.

Wittgenstein asked how one might learn the truth by thinking, and he gave his example of how this could be done, learning to see a face by drawing it. We might generalise that example by saying that thinking is a process of construction, of making something. Making, in the sense in which I have been concerned with it, is a process of thought. That is what is so: something that continues.

Notes

1 cf. T. S. Eliot, *Selected Prose*, Penguin, p. 105 (one reason for the obscurity surrounding his well-known use of this expression derives, one suspects, from its context in the essay on Hamlet, which is not among Eliot's best writing).

2 There are also obvious analogies between this view, and indeed the general direction of my argument, and the broad outlines of Collingwood's account of expression in the arts. My main difference with Collingwood, and a quite fundamental difference, is that while he has it that we are primarily dealing with emotion my own claim is that we are concerned with a process of thought. A tendency to talk of emotion or feeling where we cannot fit what we wish to describe into a standard pattern of "rational argument" is itself the main target of my general polemic.

3 cf. N. R. Hanson, *Patterns of Discovery*, Cambridge University Press, 1958; *The Scientific Book Guild*, 1962, p. 6.

4 cf. Prior, *Papers on Time and Tense*, p. 49.

5 cf. Stephan Körner, *Categorial Frameworks*, Blackwell, 1970, p. 72.

6 cf. the Introduction to Strawson's *Individuals* and S. Körner, *Fundamental Questions in Philosophy* Ch. 2, pp. 192–4. (The question is whether the clear and cogent distinctions made by these philosophers can be sustained in those areas of the subject where the philosopher's activity cannot be seen as an essentially completeable account of a static subject matter. Such a question cannot be set aside by simply allowing that there may be borderline cases between the two sorts of activities, for the question will still be what the borderline is *between*. What, in other words, will count as not on the borderline.

7 That this is so is a claim made e.g. by Stephan Körner, cf. "On some relations between logic and metaphysics", *The Logical Enterprise,* ed. Anderson, Marcus and Martin.

8 Kierkegard, *Journals* 1834–54 Fontana edition, p. 89 (May 17 1843).

I am grateful to Mr. Richard Giddens for insisting on the relevance of this passage to my argument at this point.

INDEX